HOW NOT TO BE WRONG

The Art of Changing Your Mind

JAMES O'BRIEN

You w.
Ask any men
The above does not apply to

D1420247

05383346

WH ALLEN

1

WH Allen, an imprint of Ebury Publishing,
20 Vauxhall Bridge Road,
London SW1V 2SA

WH Allen is part of the Penguin Random House group of companies
whose addresses can be found at global.penguinrandomhouse.com

Penguin
Random House
UK

First published by WH Allen in 2020
This edition published by WH Allen in 2021

www.penguin.co.uk

A CIP catalogue record for this book is available from the
British Library

ISBN 9780753557716

Printed and bound in Great Britain by Clays Ltd, Elcograf S.p.A.

The authorised representative in the EEA is Penguin Random House
Ireland, Morrison Chambers, 32 Nassau Street, Dublin D02 YH68.

Penguin Random House is committed to a sustainable future for our
business, our readers and our planet. This book is made from Forest
Stewardship Council® certified paper.

MIX
Paper from
responsible sources
FSC® C018179

For my mum, Joan O'Brien, and her granddaughters,
Elizabeth and Sophia.

'The best lack all conviction, while the worst
Are full of passionate intensity.'
W.B. Yeats, 'The Second Coming'

CONTENTS

INTRODUCTION

THERE IS NO POINT having a mind if you never change it. We should change our minds when we realise we are wrong. We realise we are wrong – or at least that we are not necessarily right – after being exposed to superior science or stronger arguments, experiences and evidence that refute our previous position. In short, by listening, thinking and learning. There should be no shame in admitting to being wrong. Instead, we should be applauded for our honesty, humility and emotional intelligence. And there should be no suggestion that admitting to being wrong about *something* somehow dilutes our overall credibility or reduces the likelihood of us being right about *anything else*.

It sounds simple and straightforward and yet it's far from easy. Pride, fear, vanity, loyalty, even our sense of self can lead us all to various positions from which it feels almost impossible to climb down. We are living in a furiously fast-moving age where our once-reliable fact-checking faculties are buckling under the sheer weight of conflicting and contradictory 'information'. The very concept of objective truth is under siege from forces that, in purely technological terms, didn't exist 20 years ago. Worse, it is a world in which empathy, perhaps second only to evidence as a catalyst for changing our minds about the most important issues, is increasingly denigrated and devalued.

All of this is rendered infinitely worse by what is perhaps best understood as the accelerating 'footballification' of public discourse. This is where we assess an action not by what has actually been done on the metaphorical pitch but instead by the shirt colour of the person who has done it. If they're on our 'team' we cheer them passionately; if they're playing for the opposition we furiously boo *absolutely identical behaviour*. As the Covid-19 pandemic swept the planet in early 2020, it quickly became clear that a widespread inability even to question the integrity of favoured political leaders, never mind the wisdom of remaining blindly hitched to their slogan-covered wagons, could quite literally have lethal consequences.

This is a book about being wrong. In it, I will try to be unflinchingly honest about my own retreats from previous positions, because I can't think of any better way to get right inside this increasingly prevalent problem of blind tribalism. In much of society today, I see open-mindedness derided as weakness, admissions of fallibility held up as evidence of deliberate dishonesty and, most incredibly, the widespread embracing of demonstrably dangerous and dishonest positions purely to upset the 'other side'. As a radio phone-in host blessed with an incredibly diverse and articulate listenership, I have been uniquely positioned to observe the drawing up of battlelines that, without a fairly profound shift in the way we discuss controversial issues, seem destined to remain in place for generations to come. It is a situation that terrifies me and makes me worry for my children's future. It is perhaps best summarised by an English caller, married to an Indian woman, who explained to me in the middle of 2019 that he knew his political hero was a liar, a racist and a fraud, but that he offered him full-throated support, that he actively 'enjoyed' being lied to, 'because it upsets people like you'. I'm still not sure precisely what he means but I hope to be closer to understanding him by the end of this book. It seems pretty clear, though, that some of the responsibility for his outwardly outrageous perspective might lie not just with people 'like' me, but with me personally.

And so this will have to be an intensely personal book and I am genuinely intimidated by this fact. For much of my life, I found it almost impossible to retreat from any position, even if I'd only arrived at it five minutes previously. I was the insufferable dinner party guest who refused to let things lie, the bloke in the pub who could never 'agree to disagree'. Looking back, it was as if I felt that being wrong would expose a vulnerability I was determined never even to contemplate, as if the foundations of my life and personality would somehow be shaken by acknowledging – even to myself – that I could be in the wrong. When I began to understand this and to search for its roots, I came to realise that I had lived much of my life in a highly adrenalised state – an almost permanent 'fight or flight' condition – and until very recently I would have been rather proud of that. These, I would have argued, are the tools that I need to be me and these reactions and reflexes are part of who I am. The crashing lows are the price you pay for the dizzying highs. Show absolute self-confidence to the world and the world will bend to your will; crush your 'enemies' *before* they mobilise and they will never be able to hurt you again. Everything is a battle and only the strongest will prevail.

It has been sobering, to say the least, to come to understand that none of it was necessary, that many of the personal attributes I took to be strengths were in fact serious and potentially very dangerous weaknesses. Now that I am able to recognise where I was going wrong, I see people with very similar mindsets and backgrounds continuing to flourish in public life and I can't help but wonder whether this weaponised 'resilience' has contributed to the current chaos and confusion on both sides of the Atlantic.

I still get the old feelings when I fall into pointless rows on Twitter (are there any other kind?). There's a bolus of tension in my gut that attributes ludicrous importance to 'winning'. The frustration felt when your rival won't admit your point, or concede defeat, brings you back for more and more until the original argument has been so clouded with confusion, claim and counterclaim that you struggle to remember what actually started it. Ten minutes later, you feel utterly ridiculous and often a bit shaky, but in the moment it felt as if nothing else mattered. In reality, of course, it really didn't matter at all. Not one jot. You will probably know someone the same; you may well be suffering similarly yourself.

As a schoolboy debater, I positively relished arguing from positions I disagreed with because it seemed a much sterner test of rhetorical skill than arguing from the head or the heart. But at some point in the intervening years, I realise now, I had begun to consider being 'right' as less important than being seen to 'win'. This pursuit of victory – of administering the knockout blow – came to completely overshadow the importance of examining my own views and understanding. I stopped, to stretch the metaphor, kicking the tyres of my own opinions because I was too busy turbo-charging the engine and congratulating myself on the latest high-speed turn around the circuit of public pontificating and arguing. Of course, the situation was hardly helped by the fact that I was building the career I thought I'd always wanted on the back of this dubious but very particular set of 'skills'. So in this book I am not seeking to persuade you that my various positions and opinions are somehow right and everyone else's wrong, but rather to show how much better it would be if none of us were unthinkingly wedded to any of them.

In many ways, my day job can be seen as both the best and the worst preparation for this process. Right across the media, a higher value is now placed on reaction than revelation. Never mind the facts, just feel the clicks. The hot take on the latest celebrity meltdown or political embarrassment has, in the 15 years I've been on the radio, seen its market value rocket. There are fortunes to be made if you can master the art of hurling verbal hand grenades into the public arena without any thought for the consequences. If you can successfully persuade yourself that migrants (or Muslims or Mexicans or female TV presenters or black politicians or 'liberals' or gays or vegans or obese people or transgender humans or students or mixed-race duchesses or teenage climate-change activists) are undeserving of the most basic human courtesies then, by encouraging others to see the world in the same way, you can currently command some of the highest salaries in the business.

Away from the so-called mainstream, ever more toxic and dishonest positions have been commoditised through YouTube advertising, Patreon appeals and other forms of 'crowdfunding'. The business model is simple and effective: send me money and I will performatively endorse your prejudices. Even better: send me money and I will tell you things that the mainstream media 'ignores' – a lucrative gambit that hinges upon knowledge that the target audience does not generally follow the news. One of the greatest ironies of our times is surely the rise of the professional complainer apparently blind to the fact that their chief complaint is that 'other people' do too much complaining. There is a grim symmetry to how any publicly declared grievance – from the climate emergency to the legacy of slavery – will spawn acres of newsprint and airtime complaining about how much time 'millennials' or the 'woke' or those pesky 'liberals' spend grumbling. Break it down like this and it's staggeringly stupid: a teenage girl complains passionately and persuasively about the catastrophic harm her elders continue to do to our planet and, like clockwork, a queue of usually old or middle-aged people forms, all moaning (for money) about how she should be quiet or sit down or go back to school. Meanwhile, the rest of us fall into silly little camps where we apparently believe either that man-made climate change is a major problem or that people complaining about man-made climate change is a major problem. Who benefits? Well, most obviously the people continuing to make huge sums of money from fossil fuels, who pay the shady 'think tanks' and 'educational charities' under a cloak of anonymity to foreground their case prominently in the British and American media.

Give them another moment and the commentators in that queue will soon be insisting that any suggestion we might all benefit from hearing less from them – and perhaps more from scientists, academics or actual 'experts' – is some sort of assault on their 'free speech'. I wrote about this in my last book, *How to Be Right in a World Gone Wrong*, but it clearly bears repeating that freedom of speech is not, as an ever increasing number of prominent people pretend to believe, the same as freedom from scrutiny.

Why do I want to lay bare the roots and results of my own often epic wrongness? The answer is twofold. Firstly, after making a massive and ongoing effort to completely change the way I look at and respond to the world I am feeling so much better about almost everything, and that has filled me with a sort of missionary zeal. Secondly, this celebration of stubbornness and our society's continuing enslavement to 'false equivalence' scare the hell out of me. If we can find more effective ways of tackling totalitarian tactics and their tragic consequences for ordinary people, we can hopefully help those people break free from the ignorance and anger which fuels the profiles and salaries of many perpetually outraged commentators and pundits – and the politicians propelled to power by their poison.

The most enthusiastic proponents of 'footballification' at its simplest cannot process the existence of people who refuse to join any team in the first place. In the context of recent British politics, for example, being deeply unimpressed by and critical of both the Conservative leader, Boris Johnson, and the former Labour leader, Jeremy Corbyn, was impossible for many to countenance. Corbyn's most committed supporters insisted that anyone unimpressed by their hero must somehow be a Tory, while Johnson's base argued that anyone who criticised him wanted Corbyn to be prime minister. The vitriol I received from both camps was often indistinguishable in tone and content. I even invented a little online game called 'Far right or Corbynite', in which I would invite readers to guess which camp an abusive message had come from. Perhaps these people need to believe that *everyone* has picked a side because it spares them the discomfort of examining their own slavish subscription to one side of a confected binary divide.

I don't know whether the decision to explore the importance of admitting to wrongness in public life would have been made if I hadn't benefitted so profoundly from addressing it in my private one. I turned out not to be quite the person I had always thought I was but, rather to my surprise at first, I found that I could make meaningful changes by properly examining why and how I'd ended up where I was.

Up until about three years ago, I had been tootling along fairly merrily, continuing to ride the usual rollercoaster of highs and lows, drink a bit too much, lose my temper too often and sometimes browbeat people around me into behaving in ways designed to make *me* feel better about what they were going through. Then one of the people I love most in the world became ill and I found, to my immense and enduring horror, I was wildly ill-equipped to provide the help and support that was both my desire and my duty. I won't get into the details here – they aren't really relevant and it is not my story to tell. The point is that a very difficult time for my family made me – eventually – wake up to the fact that thought processes and emotional reflexes that had become hard-wired into my brain as a frightened but outwardly fearless little boy at boarding school were still defining the behaviour of a middle-aged father and husband who, when push came to shove, was not proving to be as good at either role as he wanted to be.

I had been cajoling someone to somehow 'feel' better regardless of what they told me, preaching 'resilience'; insisting that *knuckling down* and *fighting harder* could somehow solve problems currently defying all manner of medicines and treatments. I tried to walk a tightrope between 'tough' and unconditional but got it horribly, dangerously wrong. I realise now that, deep down, I genuinely thought you could somehow 'argue' a poorly person better.

I saw that I had to become a better person. And for someone who has always been remarkably, although often unjustifiably, pleased with himself this was a very unexpected ambition. So I went through a process of self-examination. I talked to people who care for me and I found myself a psychotherapist. I did various things that I would have heartily scoffed at just a few years ago. And it really helped. Would I have addressed any of this if we hadn't had a family crisis? Almost certainly not. But I continue to benefit enormously from the lessons I learned, even after the crisis has mostly passed.

Did I worry that I might somehow 'therapise' myself out of an increasingly successful career by straining to be less confrontational, less combative, more understanding and more forgiving? Hell, yes. I still do, to be honest. But as our perspectives shift, so too do our priorities, and while being a verbal bruiser who routinely 'dismantles' and 'demolishes' people on the radio might work rather well in a studio designed partly to deliver 'viral clips', it is altogether less helpful in sitting rooms, symposiums and surgeries. Besides, there will always be some people who richly deserve a rhetorical roughing up – the trick is to pick your battles!

These attributes, or 'neural pathways' – best summed up as a slavish subscription to the notion that the best form of defence is attack – served me extremely well in many circumstances. I can think very quickly, identify intellectual and emotional weaknesses in others and exploit them. I have always been able to bend people to my will and spin complex webs of words. They formed a kind of suit of armour shielding me from the slings and arrows of outrageous fortune and a rapid response system which saw me always come out swinging. But, at the same time, they were clearly holding me back and even harming me in many ways. Not even the most committed knight of the Round Table would have wanted to spend his entire life in 50 kilos of full armour. And when you live always with your fists up, ready and waiting for the next attack, it hugely diminishes the space available for everything else you could be doing – and there is so, so much of that.

Weirdly, but not unhelpfully, this trauma in my personal life coincided with an astonishing, wholly unexpected surge in my professional fortunes, and no doubt prevented the epic and unbearable ego inflation that would probably have occurred if these glittering prizes had arrived in my life at any other time. On the contrary, as the book deals, ratings, media interest and public approbation I'd always dreamed of became reality, I was able to see that none of it would ever bring actual happiness and that none of it had anything to do with *who* I am. It was a difficult but important lesson in what really matters. A little perspective can go a very long way. But so, of course, can a little hubris, and no self-congratulation is intended here. I am still wrong about lots of things, I'm absolutely sure. And I'm unsure about plenty more.

One of the surest ways to change things around you is to begin by changing what's inside you. Everything from your tone of voice to your facial expressions affects people in ways that you may neither want nor understand. That sibling who always manages to rub you up the wrong way or the colleague you have to cross the room to avoid – the responsibility for these scenarios does not, indeed cannot, lie exclusively with them. Something about the way you interact with the world, whether conscious or not, contributed to the creation of an environment in which you will both be spoiling for a fight. While you can't do anything about the other person's role in this process, you can certainly do something about yours. First, you need to understand what is happening and why.

The two most important lessons I have learned while striving to be less wrong, to be happier, calmer and kinder are these: first, ask yourself, 'Where does my power lie?' when trying to work out how you should behave in a given situation. Second, 'The teacher will appear when the student is ready.' I would have sniggered at this one until very recently but, as you'll see, I've done and thought *a lot* of things I would once have sniggered at since I embarked upon this heartfelt quest.

And they mostly turned out to be of immeasurable benefit to me. That is the point of this book.

I obviously remain fallible and deeply flawed but, with the help of some remarkable experiences and people, I have come to realise that it's possible to try to be better and, occasionally, to make discoveries and changes that enormously enhance how you feel about the world and your place in it. The first steps on this path involve recognising your own wrongness and working out where it came from. That's what I want to achieve with this book, and I hope you'll find my account of tracking down and tackling the roots of my own wrongness of some use in your search for yours.

Chapter 1
IT NEVER DID ME ANY HARM

BETWEEN THE AGES OF ten and thirteen I was regularly beaten by the headmaster of my school for various alleged misdemeanours of which I was mostly, but not always, guilty. It may seem horribly at odds with modern sensibilities but it was, at least in the private school sector, unremarkable in Britain until about the mid-1980s. Rather more shockingly, until very recently I used to boast about it. A lot.

This is despite the fact that my abiding memory of being beaten is abject terror. The wait outside the headmaster's study was, if anything, more painful than the actual pain. I remember my first time quite clearly, although, perhaps pertinently, I cannot remember what apparently egregious offence I had committed. I was ten. An older boy, Joe, a veteran of this sanctioned child abuse, volunteered to go in first and I thought he had done a favour to me as a 'first-timer' – until the sound of the first 'thwack' came through the closed wooden door and turned my insides to water.

I was also, much less frequently, smacked on the backside by my mum and dad. Once or twice when my behaviour caused them to lose temporary control of themselves and, more often but still very occasionally, as a formal punishment. Either way, this was very different from what I experienced at school. I remember once feeling sorry for Dad when he got in from work, looking for nothing more than a gin and tonic and perhaps a cheeky cigar, only to be told by Mum that he had to administer a spanking because I'd committed some now unremembered crime, probably involving my sister, hours before. It's comical, really. The poor man couldn't settle down for the evening until he'd given me a light pasting for some transgression he hadn't even witnessed. He clearly didn't enjoy it either, unlike that headmaster and a few other sadistic teachers I encountered over the years.

Crucially, though, it never really occurred to him that it might be somehow 'wrong' to hit his children. It was absolutely commonplace, normal and mostly unquestioned for parents to smack kids up until about the end of the 1980s. I certainly don't blame my parents for this, but equally I would never think of smacking my own children. When I started getting paid to offer opinions on the telly I would defend the practice and argue that it *hadn't done me any harm*. There were, I think, two reasons for this. Most obviously, I love the bones of my late dad and couldn't contemplate any criticism of him. Just like Mum and most other parents, he would have died for me and my sister, and I look back on our childhood with such a sense of love, gratitude and good fortune that I felt that questioning his methods was petty and sullied his memory.

The second, less complicated reason is that I really didn't think it *had* done me any harm. Knit those two justifications together and you get a pretty neat encapsulation of why damaging patterns of behaviour so often get passed from one generation to the next. I'm increasingly convinced that one of the main reasons people with racist or homophobic views find it so hard to acknowledge and abandon their bigotries is because doing so would feel like a betrayal of a beloved parent who, for all their strengths and qualities, inculcated toxic opinions in their offspring.

The strange thing is that, unlike the beatings at school, I *still* don't think these parental punishments did me any harm. Maybe because they didn't, maybe because I can't shake the sense that to believe they did would be disloyal to my mum and dad. But even so, by the time our first child was born I had rethought my somewhat cavalier attitude to smacking children. My position had actually changed before that but my views on parenting obviously didn't make much difference to my own life until I became a parent.

My mind was changed in a TV studio in Norwich by a woman called Cathy. In 2001, I was working on a little-watched programme that nevertheless launched my broadcasting career. Every day, the host would introduce me and my co-panellist, and every day we would have heated debates about a variety of issues. I was so surprised to be there (I'd been plucked from a newspaper job that was taking an unsustainable toll on both my emotional equilibrium and my liver) and I was so keen to stay that I often agreed to argue a position I didn't necessarily hold in order to keep the programme moving. 'Taking one for the team', as it was put. On this occasion, though, I thought I was speaking from the heart. I was arguing, quite forcefully, that there was nothing wrong with a parent slapping a child if they had put themselves in danger or undertaken an act of epic disobedience.

Cathy was in the studio audience most days. This was, I discovered, because her son Gary was a recovering heroin addict and, after he moved back in with her in the hope of kicking his habit, she had determined that he needed routine in his life. Cathy worked part-time and Gary was unemployed so they were pretty skint and not exactly spoiled for choice when it came to things that would get them both out of the house with regularity and purpose. So they came to watch us.

As the weeks passed, they both became pretty frequent contributors to the studio discussions. One of the problems with a good education, I've discovered over the years, is that it can very badly blur the lines between intelligence and learning. This job, and every one I've had since that involves talking and listening to members of the public, has provided incontrovertible evidence that a good education can camouflage a relative lack of intelligence while a lack of learning can often mask extremely quick wits. Cathy was a perfect case in point. Having overcome early camera shyness, she would drop little insights and nuggets of knowledge into the conversation which often put to shame those of us being paid to be there. Writing this down, I realise what a crashing snob I must have unconsciously been. Why would I blithely presume that a woman with a broad Norfolk accent, little money and a smack addict son must also be thick and inarticulate? How embarrassing. Cathy demonstrated the gaping flaws in my presumptions.

This particular morning was among the most memorable of the whole run. I had just finished a pithy little monologue about how sometimes a slap was the only language a naughty child would understand – and I should know because few kids were as naughty as I was (pause for laughter) and, besides, it clearly hadn't done me any harm (raise eyebrow, pause for more laughter, sit back smugly and relax). Cathy had her hand in the air straight away and asked, very simply, whether I would hit my wife if she disobeyed me. Further, she wondered, would I hit her if she got on my nerves or Gary, if I saw him doing something dangerous?

I love these moments now. We call them 'penny drop moments' on the radio show and often talk of our search for the skeleton key or Rosetta Stone that can unlock the most outwardly entrenched conflicts with a single, sparkling insight. It is usually a vain quest, obviously, but my goodness it can be magical when one presents itself.

I was a different person then, though, and I tried, I think, to argue that children are unformed personalities and so in need of more robust shaping, and that it was obviously not the same. But I knew, deep down, that in some basic human way it was.

And I know now why I feel so differently about Dad punishing me compared to my headmaster. Dad loved me and didn't know that what he was doing was wrong. The headmaster, of whom more shortly, didn't love me and presumably did know what he was doing was wrong – because he never beat his own children in the same way that he beat us. Gary's estranged father, it turned out, had been particularly free with his fists when Gary was growing up and the violence had often been extended to Cathy too.

Sixteen years later, after I had become a parent myself and had it affirmed that smacking really shouldn't have a spot in the parental toolbox, a man called Andrew popped up on my show to discuss legislation in Scotland that had made it the first part of the UK to explicitly outlaw physical parental punishment. He was no more ignorant or violent than my own father, but he was stuck in a mindset that had taken Cathy's words, even more than actually becoming a dad, to free me from. The call is an almost perfect case study in what can happen when we are compelled to examine a 'wrong' opinion that we have never examined before.

Andrew: I think parents, in certain circumstances, I think they need to have that option to smack a child. And I'll give you an example: when one child hurts another child. In my case, I've got two boys and sometimes my older child would really hurt my younger child.

James: And you'd teach him that that's wrong by hurting him?

Andrew: Let me finish. This is the crux of the matter. When he'd hurt his younger brother I would have to smack him. I felt there was no option but to smack him because he needed to understand that what he'd just done – the trauma and the stress and the pain that he'd caused his younger brother – and these were very young children. However, and this was the critical thing, once that was done they'd be sent to their rooms or whatever. And an hour or so later, or the next morning, when everything had settled down and we're all happy and it's all fine and it's all forgotten about, I would call my son and I'd sit him on my knee and give him a cuddle and say, 'Now, tell me what all that was about?' And I tell you, James, we would spend an hour, sometimes even two hours, and we would almost forensically go through exactly what happened. What he did, what his brother did, how he annoyed you.

James: So it didn't work the first time, then? He didn't learn his lesson the first time?

Andrew: But children never do. They're not robots.

James: So what was the lesson, then? The lesson was that hurting people is bad and the way of teaching him this was hurting him?

Andrew: No, no, no.

James: Well, yes, yes, yes.

Andrew: But there must be a punishment, there must be a consequence.

James: We're not disputing that. Consequences are important. We're not discussing that. We're discussing teaching a child that physically hurting a child is wrong by physically hurting a child.

Andrew: I ... well ... the ... well, let me put it this way. As they got older they began to do it less and less.

James: So it happened quite a lot, then, did it?

Andrew: It would happen every so often. I mean, they couldn't stop it.

James: Well, I suppose an outsider might say ...

Andrew: Just let me finish. James, I need to say this.

James: Woah. OK. I get the picture. I'll be quiet now. Don't smack me!

Andrew: (chuckling) Nice. Nice. I would point out to him, I would say, 'Look, please you cannot do this.' I'd say, 'In our family we do not hurt each other. We don't hit each other. We don't smack each other. But I must tell you that if you hurt your brother then I will punish you for it ...'

James: I'm sorry to interrupt you, I know how much you hate it. But you just said that 'in our family we don't hurt each other'. That's not true. You hurt them.

Andrew: Yeah. Yeah.

James: So what are you saying? Are you saying, 'In our family we don't hurt each other but I will hurt you now'?

(Pause)

Andrew: If you hurt your brother.

James: So it's not true to say that 'in our family we don't hurt each other'.

Andrew: You cannot hurt your brother. You cannot harm another person.

James: But you can, though. You can harm a child.

Andrew: I would smack him, yeah, I'm telling you ...

James: There's just a slight contradiction here. Either you're not allowed to hurt people in our family or you are, and what you're teaching your kids is that *you* are but *they're* not.

Andrew wasn't a bad man and it was, in a way, quite honest of him to fall apart so quickly and completely. I hadn't been honest enough to do so when Cathy had presented me with exactly the same argument in Norwich a decade and a half previously. And that's what I thought about after he hung up.

It is very popular, in the current climate, to take facets of a person's past and use them to paint a false and unflattering portrait of their present. This, if you want, was an arrogant public schoolboy using his lucrative pulpit to browbeat a dad on national radio and make him look ridiculous. Except it wasn't. It was a dad who didn't hit his daughters sharing with a dad who did hit his sons a lesson he'd learned from the unemployed mother of a recovering heroin addict who had nothing better to do with her mornings than sit in a TV studio listening to richer, better-educated people argue about things they were sometimes only pretending to believe. And if I could learn how wrong I was from her, maybe somebody listening would learn it now from me.

Here, I suppose, endeth the first lesson. We will all need help to realise when we are wrong but, if our ears and our minds are open, it can come from pretty much anywhere. Even if you don't heed the lesson at the time.

People like Cathy and Gary and, more recently, listeners to my radio show from very different walks of life who have become firm friends over the years always make me think about my schooling and the enormous advantages it bestowed. By the time I came to understand what a huge part my education had played in my life and career it was too late to ask my dad why he had strained so hard to send me to a public school he could barely afford. For while my parents' marriage was that of equals, this was very much my dad's mission.

I realise now that it was partly formed in response to his own experiences at work. Mum explained to me once that when, in his early thirties, he arrived at the *Daily Telegraph* – hard to believe today, but at the time a glittering jewel in the crown of Fleet Street – he realised pretty quickly that his

Yorkshire accent and lack of formal education would hold him back. He determined, as Mum puts it, to buy me the 'golden ticket' with which less-talented contemporaries would breeze past him in the newspaper hierarchy. It worked.

After a shaky start and an unlikely break that involved selling a white suit to John Major, the prime minister at the time, and selling the story for some work experience shifts, I went on to become a Fleet Street section editor at the age of 26. I mention this because I remain immensely grateful for that education and acutely conscious of how lucky I was to receive it. Aside from the 'public school swagger' we will learn more of later, I would not have been able to cut my teeth as a newspaper gossip columnist if I had not been to the same school as people who routinely appeared in gossip columns. Then there are the other, more obvious benefits such as a lifelong love of literature that may not have taken root in my life if I had not been exposed to excellent teaching from an early age. With my immense gratitude to both parents and (most) teachers established, I now need to explain how, some 20 years later, I came to realise how much harm it had also done me and many other people like me. Whether we realise it or not.

My prep school in Worcestershire is under completely different ownership and management now so I won't name it here. Two of my favourite teachers from those days, who never laid a finger on me but who, back then, had reputations for being a bit too close to some of the boys, are currently serving long prison sentences for sexually abusing several of my contemporaries. My public school, Ampleforth College in the north of England, merited its own specific section in the Independent Inquiry into Child Sexual Abuse that Home Secretary Theresa May opened in 2014 and which is, at the time of writing in 2020, still hearing testimony from survivors.

Compared to the abuse described in the report I got off very lightly – though nowhere near as lightly as I'd always thought I had, as I will explain. I hope I'm not being irresponsible when I suggest that unpicking my own experiences may shed some light on why much more horrible abuses can go unacknowledged and unreported for so long. A friend, with whom I haven't yet found the courage to start this conversation, has even written about how being sexually abused by a priest most definitely did not do him any harm. A former friend and colleague once explained on air that if her own daughter were to be raped while very drunk she would not want the police to be involved but would instead give her girl a cuddle and hope that she'd learned her lesson about excessive drinking. I hope the relevance of these two examples is clear. The underlying intentions here are not to persuade you or me that being abused as a boy or raped as a young, drunk woman is no big deal. These two people are trying to persuade *themselves*. And however shocked or outraged we may be, particularly by the second example, we should obviously try to be concerned and compassionate. I appreciate this will not always be easy.

I was adamant for years that regular beatings from my prep school headmaster had not only done me no harm but had actually been a beneficial influence on my young life. I was, I think, proud of being beaten more than almost anyone else in the school's history because it burnished my rebellious credentials and, for years afterwards, I would genuinely and idiotically boast about it. It's almost impossible for me to believe now, but I also presented many radio programmes in which I would approve of grown men and women disciplining small children by leathering their little hands or backsides with a specially designed paddle. (I've often wondered where our headmaster would have gone in pre-internet days to buy his own weapon of choice. A fetish shop, probably, but we didn't have any in Kidderminster back then.) I had even constructed a policy framework to guard against abuses of the system: only one teacher should have the authority to administer physical punishment; other teachers could send pupils to him or her but not hit anyone themselves; guilt must be established beyond reasonable doubt before any punishment could occur.

It must have been clear to some people around me that I was talking utter bilge, constructing a massive edifice of self-delusion designed to deny the pain and humiliation I felt then and which I had never acknowledged or addressed since. It was a short hop from denial of the harm done to me as a form of self-protection to my arguing publicly that it was actually a good thing for little boys to be made by grown men to queue up outside their study, get beaten inside it and then, I kid you not, have to say, 'Thank you, Sir,' on the way out, straining all the while not to let him witness the tears that were, at least for the first few beatings, guaranteed to follow.

I realise now that the child's repressed feelings do not go away; they fester and ferment and end up unconsciously exerting malign and invisible influence on the adult self in ways that we often never fully appreciate. At its simplest, we deny any pain we feel to protect ourselves from the shame of acknowledging how much it hurts us. Many of us whose formative years are brutish and cruel – or at least contain episodes of brutality and cruelty – grow extra layers of skin in the hope that the barbs and stings will no longer penetrate. Think of it as a 'survival personality', a character that you need to cultivate to get by – and even to thrive – in unhealthy and unpleasant environments. And it works. That's the really tricky thing about all this. It really works. And not only may you never discover just how defined you have become by self-protection and self-defence, you may well feel great resentment towards people who point out what has happened to you. Most of us who have cultivated a 'survival personality' do not recognise or want to be told that we became what we needed to be and abandoned our authentic selves.

In April 2020, British Prime Minister Boris Johnson was hospitalised with coronavirus. His predecessor and fellow alumnus of Eton College David Cameron told *ITV News*, 'I'm sure he'll come through this,' adding that Mr Johnson was a 'very tough, very resilient, very fit person'. He explained that he derived his confidence that Johnson would not succumb to this complicated and unprecedented disease from 'facing him on the tennis court'.

I was both staggered and supremely unsurprised. I was also quite scared. I have very little time for Boris Johnson but I obviously wanted him to survive. Having just recovered from a much milder infection myself, I knew that the best way to 'fight' it was to lie down and do nothing, ideally all day and all night until you were better. The notion that toughness on a sports field could equip you with the tools necessary to rest, relax and recuperate was clearly downright dangerous. You would think it would be obvious but it really isn't.

I'm rarely surprised by the excesses of social media these days, but when I explained that talk of Johnson 'fighting' the virus like an opponent on the tennis court could actually help to kill him, the response was remarkable. I wrote:

We're taught at public school that almost any problem – illness, loneliness, being bullied, failing exams, not making the rugby team – can be fixed by 'toughening up'. These men can't help themselves – it's all they've ever known – but it's a dangerously harmful approach to life.

It turns out that people often don't thank you for pointing out truths that are a little too close to home. I was amazed when people responded by gleefully suggesting that I must have been bullied at school or not picked for the rugby team, completely missing the point. One prominent Conservative activist even suggested that I had 'inadvertently' revealed something about my own schooldays, despite the fact that I was explicitly and obviously referring to them. But when an actual government minister (these are strange times) took to Twitter to insult me in response to these heartfelt and sympathetic words it struck me just how deep the problem runs not just in people, but in society. I don't know, of course, perhaps he had a wonderful time at his private school, but the minister concerned is mixed race, so if his school was anything like others in the same era, he would have been exposed to much worse 'ribbing' than anything I ever encountered. If he had grown the extra layers of skin required to enable him to deny that any of it had ever hurt him then it appeared he wasn't looking to shed them any time soon. Fair enough. I hope he never encounters circumstances in which it would be much better for him if he did.

I gather things at these schools are now much improved, but men at schools like mine and Johnson and Cameron's were taught to face any adversity in the same way: dig deep, buck up, don't wallow, play the game, fight on, man up. And it really works. Just look at how massively over-represented alumni of the major private schools are in public life in the United Kingdom, especially England. I am not discounting nepotism, entitlement and networking from the process but, particularly in politics, 'survival personalities' seem particularly well-equipped to climb the greasy pole. The condition has a curious cousin where, rather than denying the harm done by bad experiences, a particular type of public school alumnus persuades himself that they have derived no particular benefit from their privilege. A magnificent example of this emerged when the Conservative government woefully mismanaged the handing out of A-level grades in 2020. Compelled by coronavirus to rely on estimated grades because exams could not be taken, the chosen algorithm was shown to leave pupils from disadvantaged backgrounds much more likely to have their estimate 'downgraded' and, in many cases, their university place potentially lost. One minister took to Twitter to reassure heartbroken students that 'grit and perseverance' had seen him succeed in life as opposed to exam results. He was, incredibly, a Harrow-educated Baron.

In the past, these schools created generations of men who may have been emotionally crippled but who were perfectly suited to running an empire. And it seems we are still conditioned to respect, trust and follow men who have become blind to their own pain and so, inevitably, untroubled by the pain of others. If we can pick ourselves up and dust ourselves down after a beating from a teacher or a bully then we have not surrendered or even suffered. If we can convince ourselves that it was in some way character-forming or even that we deserved it then the impact of the abuse can be hugely diluted. So it is that our 'survival personality' poses not just a risk to our own capacity for love and happiness, but also to people we come into contact with. In the case of politicians, it's a risk to entire populations.

When I clung to the notion that the privations and cruelties of my own schooling 'hadn't done me any harm' – moreover, that they had actually helped to make me 'the man I am today' – the last thing I wanted was to wonder whether that man was quite as happy and secure and 'successful' as he wanted himself, and everyone else, to believe. Whether it's my mate arguing that being molested by a priest had no effect on him whatsoever, or me explaining that I actually deserved 'the whack', or that I only got beaten up at school because I was such a cocky little fellow, it's a way of avoiding looking into ourselves and examining what we really feel. We don't have to admit that they've hurt us and we can hide, wrongly but so powerfully, how much damage they have done to us.

There was a PE teacher at my prep school, a decent bloke as it happens, who never hurt or interfered with any of us (God, what a low bar for praise that is when you think about it). He had a catchphrase designed to get us back on to the rugby field as quickly as possible after a clatter. 'It's only pain,' he would holler. 'It doesn't really hurt.' I hadn't thought of that phrase for 30-odd years until just now, as I sought the words to describe the conversations ten-year-old me had with himself about the physical beatings that I received from my prep school headmaster, as well as other teachers, and the emotional agonies that would engulf me later.

In the short term, denial dilutes everything. Everybody else may know that you're lying but as long as you never acknowledge it to yourself, you can keep a lid on the truth: it is pain.

And it really, really hurts. Physically, mentally and emotionally. And then, 20 years later, you're on daytime television delighting in the audience's cheers when you explain your support for corporal punishment – because 'it's the only language some children understand and I should know because I was one of those children!' – on a show dedicated to the sort of confected debate that has latterly come to dominate public discourse. And then wondering, in those rare moments when the armour falls away, why it all feels so hollow.

These days, I would argue that an astonishing amount of public 'debate' is driven and defined by people who have, like me, constructed personas of denial and projection designed to show the world a facade that bears little resemblance to what lies within. I used to wax lyrical about how many outwardly homophobic people were secretly ashamed of their own sexuality, and those shiny-faced American TV evangelists will keep proving the point, but I was in my mid-forties before I understood that I also operated in my very own state of denial.

What begins as an unconscious self-defence mechanism ends up defining our attitudes to so many things, not just opinions and issues, but also relationships, people and even life itself. To realise this about oneself is as shocking as it is liberating. And, as I discovered when I was forced to recognise that my own survival personality – my 'Come on! Try harder! You can beat this' attitude – was not just useless but actively harmful to my family and myself, the first thing you have to do is be honest with yourself. Though it turned out that I couldn't do it; I literally couldn't see that my response to all adversity was as wrong as it was ingrained. I'm still ashamed to admit that it was also doing harm to someone I love more than life itself and who couldn't 'fight' their illness any more than Boris Johnson could 'fight' a coronavirus with tennis tactics. But I couldn't see that either. So, reluctantly, somewhat desperately and mostly at my wife's behest, I found myself a therapist.

Chapter 2
STIFF UPPER LIPS

WE STILL CALL THEM 'trick cyclists' at work. Psychologists, psychotherapists and psychiatrists are all lumped together in the minds of many media professionals as practitioners of weird pseudo-science whom we can wheel out to provide a few words about the motivation of a serial killer or the likely childhood background of a terrorist. I didn't quite have their efforts filed in the same category as coffee enemas and homeopathy but it was close. Against this backdrop, it would be fair to say that I didn't exactly approach my first therapy session with enthusiasm. There was hope of sorts but it was very much of the 'I'll try *absolutely anything* if there's even the vaguest chance of it making me more useful to my family – even a coffee enema!' variety.

I filled in a short form about my habits and behaviour and realised just how much alcohol I had started drinking in the hope, I suppose, of securing temporary reprieves from reality. Not as much as I had in my newspaper days but rather more than I had for quite a few years. I presumed that this would be the focus of my 'treatment' but, to my absolute horror, in the session in which the therapist and I were both to decide whether or not we wanted to proceed with the process, she instead began talking about the importance of looking after the child I used to be. The child I used to be? Crikey. Sitting nervously in a charming little studio at the bottom of a garden in west London, I was told that I might soon be having actual conversations with my younger selves and writing letters to teachers who had hurt me. I very nearly burst out laughing.

Three things need to be stressed here. First, I am a beneficiary of therapy and am in no way qualified to advise anyone else. As I now have first-hand experience of its benefits, I wish it was more widely available and I hope that one day it will be. Second, I was incredibly lucky to fall into the care of a brilliant and perfectly suited practitioner. This is not always the case. Third, I really cannot exaggerate how completely cynical, sceptical and dismissive of the whole business I used to be.

Callers to my radio show and experiences outside work had, by about 2017, at least set me straight on the reality and prevalence of depression and anxiety. Before that, I really was a fully paid-up member of the 'pull your socks up' brigade. I would, if pushed, have even accused sufferers of skiving and malingering and, quite frequently, claimed that my generation had somehow been raised 'stronger' than succeeding ones. I would even argue that conditions such as attention deficit hyperactivity disorder were just fancy euphemisms for 'naughty'. (And I should know, right, because I used to be sooo naughty ...)

I didn't burst out laughing during that first session. I was there because I was desperate. We talked about the fact that I was adopted as a baby and had been 'sent away' to school and, she explained, these two factors would often engender feelings of abandonment and fears of rejection. I was quietly outraged at this and couldn't help but hear it as criticism of my parents. Mum and Dad loved the bones of me and everything they had done for me had come from the very bottom of their hearts. My biological mother had given me up because she knew that she couldn't provide me with the life she felt I deserved. I was actually luckier than most children because I had been 'chosen' and so desperately wanted. These statements were articles of faith for me. They were, I was certain, part of my very being. I hadn't been 'abandoned' or 'rejected'. What ridiculous suggestions. But the more I talked (as a radio presenter I know how effective silence can be because the interlocutor feels compelled to fill it, but I was entirely on the receiving end of this now) the more I came to see and feel things I had never really seen or felt before.

The fundamental premise of the treatment I received is that wrongs done to us as children are the root cause of many of the things we do wrong as adults. The first and most fundamental challenge, as I understand it, is to stop believing that no wrongs were done to us. For kids like me, admitting suffering is a sign of victory for whatever forces have tried to hurt you. And if you ever sense feelings of vulnerability or hurt bubbling to the surface, you screw them back down again.

Hard. Why? Because it works. If we were capable of acknowledging and analysing it at the time, I think most of us would have argued that it was the only way to survive. And, for now at least, I still think we would have been right.

However, that was then and this was now. If my continuing failure to be the husband and father I wanted to be could be in any way rectified then I would have to listen to this woman. I would have to wonder whether being adopted and 'sent away' and beaten and emotionally abused (I still wasn't ready to admit those words applied, but that's what it was) had in fact caused me to lock away my real self and construct instead a survival personality. And if my 'real' self would really be of more use to my family, I would now obviously have to at least try to find him. Even if it meant having actual conversations with my younger selves and writing letters to teachers who aren't even alive anymore and indulging in other outwardly bonkers behaviours.

So here are two more things I was deeply wrong about. I used to think that the sort of mental conditioning we're examining here was unique to British public schools and I used to believe – hilariously, in retrospect – that I had completely avoided it. I remember reading *Enemies of Promise* by the author and critic Cyril Connolly when I was about 15. I only withdrew it from the library because it was quoted at the front of one of my favourite plays of the time. It wasn't my usual fare. I was more typically hopping between Jane Austen, J.D. Salinger and James Herbert then, but I had been completely entranced by a film called *Another Country* starring an unknown Colin Firth and Rupert Everett, who had *actually been to my school!* (Furthermore, in a perfect example of behaviour that my children insist should not be excused on the grounds of different values applying to different eras but which I still think of quite fondly, a performatively camp old English teacher had once stated that 'James O'Brien's Bottom is the finest thing to grace the Ampleforth stage since Rupert Everett's Titania.')

So I bought a copy of the play the film was based on and was dumbstruck by the Connolly quote that the playwright Julian Mitchell had put on the frontispiece. It described what Connolly, a contemporary of George Orwell's at Eton, had termed his 'Theory of Permanent Adolescence', which he described as follows:

It is the theory that the experiences undergone by boys at the great public schools, their glories and disappointments, are so intense as to dominate their lives and to arrest their development. From these it results that the greater part of the ruling class remains adolescent, school-minded, self-conscious, cowardly, sentimental, and in the last analysis homosexual.

I would, for the record, disagree pretty profoundly with the final word of his conclusion (the play is partly about a gay love affair) but the rest still rings remarkably true. It's stirring stuff and was proof, to my teenage self, that some of the other big names on campus, mostly the sportsmen and the prefects, were emotional cripples who could only dream of the inner lives and emotional riches that me and my artistic, theatrical and literary friends enjoyed. It would be about 30 years before I came to see not just that *I* was crippled, but also that many of them were not.

These days, I find the whole concept of boarding schools quite troubling, but the majority of children who pass through them can clearly benefit enormously from the education and even the pastoral care available. Some of us, for whatever reason, feel a need to live our lives on a bigger stage than everyone else – at school they were the show-offs, the attention seekers, the boys who wanted to run the empire or be famous or prime minister when they grew up. Connolly was describing them, I think, not the lads who happily got on with getting on with it.

As the responses to that tweet in the last chapter referencing tennis tactics and lethal diseases demonstrated, there are two types of people who deny the damage that this sort of schooling can do and it is, at first, almost impossible to tell them apart. Are they in denial about the very existence of their own survival personality or are they just telling the truth about having had a relatively healthy time at school and can't imagine (or acknowledge) that someone else had a different experience? I'm pretty good at spotting the difference now but it took me some time. The reason this still matters so much is, of course, because the make-up of these 'ruling classes' in Britain today remains pretty much identical to when Connolly described them almost a hundred years ago.

I want you to meet some people from the same country but a completely different world. Lee is a 35-year-old bike courier and former gang member. Most of his life had involved criminality and violence, but when he rang me in response to a question about how hard it is to avoid gang culture in urban Britain, I was quite staggered to find myself thinking of Connolly's Theory of Permanent Adolescence. It still brings tears to my eyes. Obviously, one feels enormous sympathy for all victims of violence and the drug trade, and inevitably many people respond to tales like Lee's by asking, 'What about the victims?' As with so much else, it's not either/or. We really don't have to pick a side and if we are serious about wanting to stop it, we probably shouldn't.

James: What's your story, Lee?

Lee: I'm out of it now, you know, I've had help. A lot of help.

James: Who from?

Lee: Um. From people I know, from people who say, 'Lee, you really can't be doing that now,' and as I get older I kind of understand how wrong it was, you know, but when you're young you're just in the moment.

James: But there must have been kids when you were young who didn't go down this route?

Lee: There was, yeah.

James: So what was the difference between them and you?

Lee: I think they were more clever kids, do you know what I mean? They were able to work out what they wanted. We was kind of like followers but they were able to work out what they wanted to do. But not every kid ... not every kid ...

(Lee's voice, to my complete surprise, starts breaking here.)

Lee: People don't even know at 35 what they want to do, let alone at 16, you know? At 16 you still don't know what you want to do so you just follow the gang down that road, you know?

James: Because it's the path of least resistance?

Lee: It might even be in your block of flats. For you to come, for you to come out of your front door, you've got to go past these people. So if you're not with them you're going to get beatings every day.

James: Just for refusing to join in? And when I say 'join in', I don't mean just standing with them on the street corner. I mean actually going with them to rob people or whatever?

Lee: Yeah. Even if you're just standing there and don't actually give the person a wallop, you're still part of it. You're just a number. You're still part of the fear that the opposing [gang member] feels because there are ten of you and you're one of that number.

James: So you turn on a radio programme like this and you hear people talking about gangs and gang culture and you hear them talking about it as if it's about some sort of alien species. The way you describe it to me, it's a hell of a lot easier to go down the path you went down than it is to steer clear if you come from that sort of background?

Lee: Right. What I'm saying is right now, like I said to you, I'm out of it now, yeah? Right now, I drive a motorbike and I'm telling you now, James, I drive a motorbike and I just about survive, yeah? I go out there and do a bit of couriering and try and get my money that way because I ain't got the cleverness for all these jobs, you know? Because I went down the wrong path. And then I get a ticket ...

(Lee's voice starts breaking again here and, again, at the time I couldn't understand why.)

Can you imagine I go out there and I'm busting my guts trying to get these parcels delivered to the people and I'm making my money, but I'm making it the proper way now, and then, and then, it brings me to tears it really does ...

James: Go on, mate. Take your time.

Lee: You know, like. Sorry, I'm sorry ...

James: That's alright. Take your time. You've got all the time you need. I promise.

(Pause.)

Lee: Ah. Sorry, man. Sorry. Gotta go.

James: No, Lee, just give me another minute, because what you're trying to tell me is that you're trying to do your best, you're playing by the rules, and something flies into your world like a parking ticket or a speeding fine and it takes such a big chunk out of your income that you wonder why you're doing it.

Lee: (crying now) Correct. Correct. What am I doing it for? What am I doing it for? I was better the other way, wasn't I? You know? I was better the other way.

James: No, you weren't.

Lee: I was better the other way.

James: Can I ask you a question you don't have to answer? When you were in the middle of the gang stuff how much money were you making a week?

Lee: Maybe about four hundred, something like that.

James: So you were never exactly rolling in money?

Lee: No. I was never rolling in it. You've got to pay the boss man, you know, you've got to pay the boss man.

James: But now you feel that you're constantly on the verge of the wheels coming off, metaphorically speaking?

Lee: Correct. Correct. You know?

James: I've never heard this before. I'm going to level with you. This idea that you're doing the right thing but no one really understands how hard it is to do the right thing. Because you could just take one step back into the old life and you'd have a few hundred quid clear at the end of every week.

Lee: (sobbing) Correct. Correct. The right feels like the wrong, you know, and the wrong feels like the right these days, man. You know?

(Pause.)

Lee: (whispering) You know?

James: (sighs) I do. I do now. I didn't before.

Lee: (sobbing) That's what it feels like out here, man.

James: I get that now.

James: And anyone who says to you, 'You've made the right choices, Lee, you've done the right thing' – these are just words.

Lee: Exactly. But I owe so much to the people who've helped me, man.

James: (struggling now to find any words of use to Lee) Well, that's what you've got to focus on. The debt you owe to the people who've helped you. You just need someone to put some trust and love in like they've put trust and love in you.

Lee: (sobbing) Exactly. Exactly, man. I gotta go, man. I'll see you, man.

I don't know what happened to Lee. I hope he's OK. I'm not embarrassed by our exchange and the obvious inadequacy of my 'advice', but I would speak to him rather differently today. At the point in our conversation when his voice started breaking – when the pent-up emotion first got the better of him and he briefly remembered his 16-year-old self and acknowledged the struggles he had had – I would tell him that he needs to forgive himself, to promise that 16-year-old boy that he is safe now and that grown-up Lee will look after him. I would tell him, in other words, that he needs to have an actual conversation with his younger self . . .

Listening back now, Lee seems on the cusp of either trying (without the benefit of often expensive therapy) to shed the layers of thick skin he'd grown to survive or retreating back into them and returning to a life that was clearly brutal and wrong. He sounds, to me, like a man who sees the scars of his youth as the only protection against the travails of his adulthood.

The multi-award-winning rapper Dave, whose work draws heavily on his experiences of gangs while growing up in the south London suburb of Streatham, and so could hardly be further away from the playing fields of Eton, puts it quite perfectly in his track 'Psycho', which opens with him apparently beginning a course of psychotherapy and goes on to examine why he doesn't want it. He rejects his teacher's suggestion that he seek counselling because he feels he needs 'so many old scars' to survive. He doesn't want to 'heal'.

I would have said the same once, albeit less lyrically and drawing on an outwardly very different set of experiences. When you spend your formative years expecting an attack from any angle – whether it's from members of a rival gang, school bullies or a sadistic headmaster – you don't notice what it's done to you until the process of self-protection is complete. You spend life with your metaphorical fists up, lashing out at the mildest provocation in a way that will seem freakishly over the top to others.

For me, it was obviously verbal blows that I rained down on anyone who shook my entirely confected sense of certainty about the world and my place in it. I don't mean shouting and bellowing, although there was some of that; I mean deploying my 'gift' for making people feel small and stupid in order to shore up the often false notion that I was 'right' and they were 'wrong'. It's a 'gift' that *might* help make you an effective boss or an excellent sports coach or a successful businessman, but though it equips you to do battle it robs you of any ability to recognise moments when it will be not just useless but actively harmful.

And so I found myself squaring up to a profound and frightening problem with the only weapons I'd ever known, which were quite spectacularly unfit for purpose. From school to the casual brutality of a tabloid newsroom, verbal dexterity and quick wits, with a side order of crushing cruelty, had seen me successfully through all the major battles of my life. It would not see me through this one, and yet I could literally not conceive of any other way to address it.

Of course, you cannot 'fight' the sort of problems my family faced any more than you can 'fight' a coronavirus, but I remained completely incapable of understanding this until I acknowledged that I had been deeply hurt by things I'd spent a lifetime describing as 'character-forming'. I had built a mythology around myself that not only denied this hurt but also insulated me against the impact of future attacks. Our skin is never thicker than when scarred, and in order to begin the process of shedding my own scars, I would have to acknowledge and address the wounds that had caused them.

The Arsenal and England footballer Ian Wright, like Lee and Dave, could hardly have had a more different upbringing than my own. An abusive stepfather and an emotionally absent mother conspired to create a frightened but outwardly fearsome character who would also greet every situation with his fists up – although in his case not metaphorically. I know this because, just as I was wrestling with the question of how much I should share here of my own experiences with therapy, he popped up on my radio speaking with incredible candour and emotion about his own.

For most people, the most remarkable element of his BBC *Desert Island Discs* episode would be his tearful memories of a teacher, Sydney Pigden, who was the first and for a long time the only person who made his younger self feel valued and loved. It was raw, heartbreaking testimony, all the more so because outwardly Wright has always been every inch a 'man's man'. For me, those tears were a window on the boy he used to be, a boy he had been compelled to abandon and forget in order to be 'tough' and 'resilient'. What resonated most was his description of how he had managed to stop being the short-tempered and often violent man he had become in order to cope with the pain of his own childhood experiences. He said:

I needed therapy. I'd got to a stage in my life where you're not hearing the word 'No' because you're doing so well and that's dangerous to the point you're obnoxious. I went to see this wonderful woman and she recognised after the first few sessions [and said]: 'You're not telling me the truth – why have you come here? If you want to waste money go and do it somewhere else because I've got too many people who need help and you are wasting my time.' She said that and then I burst into tears … and then I poured it all out and the therapy was the best thing that ever happened to me. What I realised was that a lot of it stemmed from my youth and when I was a child. One time she asked me about being hugged. She said, 'Can you remember the first hug you got from your mum? Can you remember any time your step-dad showed you affection?' And I literally couldn't remember anything like that.

It made me realise that it wasn't great when I was growing up but I turned it into something and I'm just pleased that I got to a stage … I didn't want to be that guy that when I looked in the mirror I didn't like myself.

This realisation that, despite outward 'success', you have become someone that you neither want nor need to be is so incredibly liberating that it's hard to put into words. Wright does a better job here than I have.

I should add that when I told Ian that his courage and clarity had inspired me to try to be just as honest about my own, very different, experiences, his encouragement was as sensitive as it was inspiring. I remain incredibly grateful. It was his line about looking in the mirror that did for me. This simple but immeasurably huge admission that you just don't like what you are and really want to be something, someone else. As a person who had always rather revelled in my reputation for being far too fond of myself, this was quite a revelation.

I cried a lot too as my treatment progressed. So much so that it's hard to remember instances specifically. It began with the burning, screwed-down sadness of my family situation, my unacknowledged powerlessness to make everything better, the suppressed but constant knowledge that I was actually making things worse. I cried for my children and my wife and, of course, for myself. And amid all this scattergun sobbing I started to cry for the little boy standing outside his headmaster's study, his insides turned to water at the thought of the agonies ahead. I cried for the lad who phoned home from boarding school to tell his mum and dad how splendidly everything was going when in reality he was so crushingly, unspeakably, constantly lonely. I cried for the teenager who had become such a big, overbearing personality that he was never off stage, always scrapping with older boys or teachers or his housemaster, but who, privately, just wanted to curl up in his mum's lap at a home hundreds of miles away. I cried for the young man who had somehow persuaded himself that all criticism, however hurtful, was really a compliment and that you couldn't enjoy delirious highs in life without enduring crushing lows. And as I cried for him, he came back to me. In all those myriad guises.

It was the strangest, most magical experience of my life, and for a while I dared not think about it too deeply. There's a line I always remembered from a letter John Keats wrote, 'O for a life of sensations rather than of thoughts!' It makes perfect sense to me now. I needed to somehow turn off my brain, with all its analysing and explaining and excusing, and focus everything on my feelings, but I don't think I could have done it consciously. I needed to be mugged by it.

'Tell him how you feel,' said the therapist. 'Imagine ten-year-old you now, sitting next to you on this sofa, and tell him whatever you want.'

'I'm sorry,' I said, without pausing or thinking or remembering just how silly I was supposed to find this sort of thing. 'I'm so, so sorry. But I'm here now and I will never let them hurt you again. I promise you. You're safe now. They will never hurt you again.'

To discover in your mid-forties that you have lived your whole life being completely and utterly wrong about who and what you are is, to say the least, a bit of a surprise, but it proved remarkably easy to process. It was so obviously *true* that it brooked no challenge. The therapeutic process doesn't work for everyone, and even when it does not everyone will necessarily feel the foundations of their very existence shift as profoundly as I did, but there was simply no arguing with how freed I felt. If you have ever suffered from insomnia, you will recognise the simple beauty of finally feeling the approach of sleep. It's like balm. Imagine living your whole life with a rotten tooth but not knowing that there was anything unusual about the situation. You would think it normal to eat on one side of your mouth, to regularly poke the infected area with your tongue, to live your entire life in ways designed to avoid a stab of pain. And then one day, the tooth is gone. It changes how you feel about everything.

Self-improvement is a work constantly in progress, impossible to complete and easy to slip back from. But once you are aware of this new, right way of living and feeling, it's always there. The knot of fear and tension in my stomach that had been pretty much my permanent companion since the age of about 15 was not actually part of me. It was a scar and it could heal. Interestingly, for me at least, I noticed around this point that I had stopped biting my fingernails (and I went for the proper, bloody, cuticle-shredding approach) for the first time since childhood.

The next task involved writing to the men who had buried the boy I used to be and done more than anyone else to turn me into a man I didn't want to see in the mirror any more. I had carried my warped philosophy of self-protection from little school to big school where, though no longer involving physical pain, my experiences turned out to have been even more damaging than the beatings. I am going to reproduce the letters I wrote to my prep school headmaster and public school housemaster in full here. I've changed some, but not all, the names. I never sent them – one of them is dead anyway – as I didn't see the point. Writing them helped *me* enormously and no longer had anything to do with *them*. But I want you to read them now because they provide a much better illustration of how all this worked than anything else I could write here. And also because such experiences are, of course, still very much a part of what makes up those 'ruling classes'. The language is a bit ripe, some of it you already know, there's a reference which only fans of the Kevin Dillon film *Catholic Boys* could possibly appreciate and even I was surprised at the depth of anger that came pouring out. What was most amazing for me, when writing them, was the way in which my adult voice seemed to revert back to those of my 13- and 18-year-old selves. I didn't go to war. I wasn't raped by the photography teacher. I came from a comfortable, middle-class family where love was boundless. The point, I suppose, is that if I can carry scars like these through my life then so can absolutely anyone.

Dear Simon,

My beautiful daughters are ten and twelve now but they are still, in the great scheme of things, tiny. I was seven when I came into your orbit and almost immediately associated you with fear and pain. I remember Miss Johnson, in my first term at **********, threatening to send me to the headmaster because I had used a rude word I did not know the meaning of in class. I remember crying and being terrified that I would get the 'whack' as a result. It would be three or four years before I actually found myself standing outside your study listening to you beat a classmate, knowing that I was next. I smile at the memory of Joe Bruce pushing me out of the way so he could go first because, as an already experienced recipient of your abuse and violence, he knew that standing outside was in some ways worse than being inside. At the time, I thought he was doing me a favour.

You were, of course, a grown man. You must have been at least six foot three, you were a strong man and you owned a small rubber paddle which had presumably been designed for the purpose of hitting people, in your case small children. Where the fuck do you buy something like that? Soho? There was no internet back then so you must have gone to some trouble. Perhaps you inherited it from your father, who was also a nasty bastard 'famed' for the unpredictability of his beatings. It is a mark of how much better a man I am than you that the thought of him kicking the shit out of you as you once kicked the shit out of me makes me feel at least some sympathy for you.

Because your violence and brutality were not confined to formal beatings, were they Simon? They were part of your vocabulary of terror and tyranny. You were a grown man, a husband and father of four, who ruled over boys aged between seven and thirteen – many of whom would board at the school and not see their homes or parents for weeks on end – with fear and brutality.

Off the top of my head, I remember the time we were ordered to spend our weekend spare time doing manual labour for you, shifting furniture. We weren't being punished, we were simply doing unpaid grunt work. Bizarrely, we did *Nicholas Nickleby* as the school play around this time but I didn't realise then that you were no better than Wackford Squeers, the bastard headmaster I played who treated the children in his charge like animals. On this occasion, messing around with my mates, I let go of my corner of a big table that four of us were carrying and I was laughing when, completely out of the blue, you came up behind me and kicked me up the backside so hard that I left the ground and landed on the floor. I couldn't sit straight for a week. This was, it astonishes me to remember, a perfectly ordinary occurrence.

When Mr Brown, who I realise now was suffering from severe mental problems, beat me up very badly in front of horrified parents on Bonfire Night you were temporarily terrified that your school, your money-spinning business, was in existential danger. My beloved father, whose shoes you were not fit to lace, elected not to press charges or go public because, bless his memory, he didn't want me to be followed around by the story at my next school and even for the rest of my life. It was a few weeks later that, having 'caught' me messing around in an unsupervised classroom, you announced to everyone present that I'd better behave or 'I'll do a Mr Brown on you and by God you won't get up again'. Mr Brown had punched me in the face so hard with his clenched fists that the bruises took weeks to heal. So you'd seen them every day and still said this to me. I'm pretty sure that this was the day I was due to travel to Ampleforth to sit the scholarship exam so it's not even as if we can offer up you being a decent headmaster in mitigation for you being a despicable human being. You were shit at both.

I remember the violence you visited on others. There was my friend who went off the rails when his parents divorced and my friend who probably got beaten more often than me and who was, we now know, being regularly abused by the photography teacher. How could it not have occurred to you that his serial misbehaviour might be symptomatic of a deeper malaise? Your contribution to his unspeakable suffering was to regularly beat him for misbehaviour and disobedience. What a fucking joke you are.

I saw you in my church before you died. One of your children must live nearby. I heard you ask the priest about christening your grandson. I love the fact that you could not look me in the eye, that my father's son had achieved so much more in life than your father's son ever did or ever will and I wonder still whether I should have wandered over and asked how old your grandson would have to be before you began beating him like you beat me and Jason and Ben and Joe and hundreds of other boys. But I didn't. Because your children didn't deserve that any more than we deserved to be abused by you.

James O'Brien

Dear Felix,

You will, I know, be surprised to learn that I think of you now with nothing but disgust. You see yourself, no doubt, as a man who exercised benign influence over the boys in your charge but take it from me: you were an evil bastard and almost certainly still are. Some of us were too thick or too groomed to appreciate the extent of your malign influence, Felix, but not me. Never me.

My mum, who saw my arriving at Ampleforth as a glorious vindication of her and Dad's whole lives, told you that I was adopted on the day that she dropped me off for the first time.

She told you that she didn't want you to tell me that you knew but thought it best that you be prepared for any problems it might throw up while I was at school 250 miles away from a woman who knew more about unconditional love than you ever will.

It took you about a month to call me into your study one evening – in many ways a welcome invitation because it was the only room we ever encountered that actually felt a bit homely – and announce that you knew I was adopted and that in your experience adopted boys came to look upon *you* as their real father. What sort of a sick fuck could betray a mother's trust like that? Think about this, Felix. My mother and father believed, wrongly I now know, that you and your school could somehow provide me with a more valuable environment in which to grow up than they could. Partly because of my dad's faith and, I smile as I write this, partly because of my mum's social aspirations, they thought that a place like Ampleforth and monks like you would provide something almost magical to a lad like me. You took that trust, that belief, and you shat all over it.

What were you thinking, man? That I wouldn't immediately call my mum and tell her what had happened? I became a 'rebel' that day because I knew, somewhere inside, that you were a fraud and a charlatan. It culminated in me breaking my parents' hearts by being expelled but how the fuck was I supposed to respect authority when authority was embodied by you? You didn't seem so keen to adopt a fatherly role in my life when the Humberside drug squad were scaring the bejaysus out of my 18-year-old self. You didn't apologise, you didn't take responsibility for betraying their trust so completely.

I realised when Dad died just how acute the financial sacrifice involved in sending me there had been and how he'd never really recovered from the economic impact of being made redundant in my final year. I was astonished to discover that I could hate you more than I already did. But I remember when relations between us had broken down almost completely and you wrote to him trying, I realise now, to persuade him to take your side in your ongoing attempt to bury my personality under an avalanche of conformism and forelock-tugging. He saw through you, Felix, just as I had all those years before and he put you in your place in the most glorious manner. I remember you reading me the letter he sent you telling you, in more moderate terms, to fuck off and I remember you attempting to portray an amused confusion at his words, but I saw that you had nothing to offer up against an unbreakable bond between a real father and son. And I saw that you knew it. You had a glimpse of what paternal love really is and it confounded your curdled soul. Even when I was expelled he was there for me, putting me first, hiding his heartbreak and disappointment. My dad was a quiet man, but a fierce one when the occasion demanded it. He could have chewed you up and spat you out but he didn't – because he was putting me first as usual. Part of me wishes that he hadn't.

I survived. I strapped on my armour every day and went off to battle, often against you. I took my teenage sensibilities, matched them with your adult ones, and mostly prevailed. But at what cost? I'm not going to be the boy waiting for his next joust with you and people like you any more. I'm hanging up my lance. I have so much in my life but I'm greedy. I want more. I want to be a better dad and a better husband, a better friend and a better son and I know that simply by shrugging off the shell you made me grow I'll be halfway there. Because here's the thing, 'Father' Felix, real men don't measure themselves against children. They look after them. Like my dad did. Like I do. Like you couldn't.

Dominus Vobiscum, shithead.

James

You could, of course, have gone through everything that I went through and emerged completely differently. You might have had a childhood as loveless as Ian Wright's without growing into an angry, self-loathing adult. You could have walked out of Lee's block of flats as a teenager and somehow steered clear of the dangers that engulfed his life or even endured them without being left so scarred. Of course you could. And maybe being told to dry your eyes and pull your socks up and keep your upper lip stiff has served all of us well at some point. But it has also caused harm. And you cannot heal that harm by pointing out that somebody over there is in a lot more pain. It is profoundly wrong to try to diminish or dismiss one person's pain by pointing out that another person has suffered 'more'.

This, I soon learned, had become one of the most obvious and easily identifiable negative traits of my own survival personality. For as long as I can remember, I would try to console myself by thinking that, however bad I might feel, things could be much worse. It's a form of denial designed, I think, to keep you afloat in the short term, but which will, in the long term, shut down any temptation to examine and so hopefully heal our pain. It becomes a neural pathway, a behaviour that feels reflexive and natural but is actually learned and rather unnatural. And it all stems from seeing those scars and stiff upper lips as strengths, from thinking that you need to deny and distract yourself from what you carry deep inside from your past in order to be effective and successful in the present.

I find it hard to believe now, not least because it really wasn't very long ago, but I would genuinely see, 'Well, at least it's not terminal,' as a 'helpful' response to somebody's serious, life-changing illness. Worse, I was so tied up in managing and manipulating my own deeper feelings that I would, I realise now, be completely blind to other people's. When you carry a bolus of tension and dread in your tummy on an almost permanent basis, without thinking for a moment that there is any other way to live, so much of your life becomes unwittingly enslaved to it. I would constantly ask my wife, 'Are you alright? Is everything OK?' for two reasons, neither of them linked in any way to sincere concern for her wellbeing. First, when your survival personality has conditioned you to be on permanent adrenalised guard, you are constantly seeking reassurance that there is no new attack on the horizon. And by 'attack' I don't mean the slings and arrows of schools and workplaces, I simply mean bad news. You are seeking reassurance that nothing bad is about to happen despite the fact that nobody could ever provide it. Second, when you are so tightly strung, every criticism or quibble *feels* like an attack and so prompts a completely inappropriate response. You *think* you are trying to make the other person feel better but it is *actually* all about you. I wasn't enquiring after my wife's wellbeing; I was asking her to confirm that there weren't any more catastrophes incoming. Please reassure me, please make me feel better, please alleviate the tension in my gut, please take away the fear.

The simple, obvious truth is that only you can do any of those things. This, I think, is the point of therapy. At least, that's how it worked for me. I thank my lucky stars every single day that I found it when I did. Of course, if you'd told me even four years ago that I would be believing and writing about things like these I would have laughed in your face and sent you away with a coffee enema in your ear.

Chapter 3
STOP AND SEARCH AND ECHO CHAMBERS

IT IS RATHER POPULAR at the moment to describe any-body with whom you disagree as inhabiting an 'echo chamber' that prevents them from seeing the error of their ways – and, of course, the incontrovertible correctness of your own. The idea is that people deliberately avoid any views or opinions that challenge their own worldview and instead surround them-selves with the like-minded. You might think that presenting a daily radio phone-in programme, where dissent and disagree-ment are not just encouraged but often sorely needed, would insulate me from the accusation, but you'd be wrong. Instead, the 'echo chamber' allegation is simply the newest weapon designed to spare us the inconvenience of thinking for our-selves by silencing everyone who encourages us to do so. Ask-ing someone to explain themselves is an attack upon their 'freedom of speech' and the attacker invariably inhabits an 'echo chamber'. As with most practices that can, on closer examination, look like baby steps toward totalitarianism, there is a heavy dose of projection involved. In my experience, the person most likely to accuse others of inhabiting an echo chamber is in fact the person most terrified of examining or explaining their own opinions, whether through a buried sense of shame or simply suppressed knowledge of their flimsiness. You almost certainly know a prime example.

The surest way to break down these chamber walls is to listen not just to people possessed of very different opinions but, crucially, to people possessed of profoundly different experiences. I realised after a few years on air – and long before my own deeply personal wrestles with my past led me to see much of the world in a coruscating new light – that *experiences* are worth a million times more than *opinions* when we come to assess what is 'right' and what is 'wrong'. Inevitably, the issue which brought this home to me with a staggering strength was one of which I had precisely no previous personal experience: stop and search.

Known as stop and frisk in America, this policing tactic sees people, overwhelmingly young black men, stopped in public on little or no grounds and ordered to prove they do not possess drugs or weapons by emptying their pockets and being searched. When I began broadcasting, I was all in favour of it. Such is the nature of the British media that, incredibly, this middle-class white man who had never experienced stop and search – but who had actually been in trouble with the police for drug use – was paid actual money to explain why it was right to subject blameless young black men to the practice on the grounds that 'if you've got nothing to hide, you've got nothing to fear'. I also now think that there was an echo of the 'it didn't do me any harm' mythology behind this. I accepted that excessive and often indiscriminate 'discipline' by authority must be a good thing because to admit that it wasn't would be to run the risk of admitting the harm it did me personally, albeit in a wildly different context.

The next line in this paragraph may well prove to be wrong, but that's partly the point of this book – to expose my own views to harsher scrutiny than I can manage alone. I don't think I encountered any 'real' racism growing up. I knew about the 'No Dogs, No Blacks, No Irish' signs in boarding house windows but they seemed to me to belong to a different age. And I was all too familiar with the conflation of Irishness with support for Irish Republican terrorism but I just didn't see it as 'racism'. Not least because it was all so obviously rubbish while 'racism' was, for me, so obviously serious.

The headmaster I told you about would occasionally make derogatory comments about 'the Irish' and boys with apostrophes in their name seemed to get 'disciplined' more than the average, but I don't think any of us – the O'Briens, the O'Reillys, the O'Mahonys – felt particularly victimised because he would also pick on our peers for being, variously, ginger-haired, overweight, bespectacled or a little bit slow on the uptake. I have a very vague memory from when I was seven or eight of another teacher nicknaming an older Asian pupil 'Dusky', partly because his surname was a similar-sounding word, but I can't think of any other examples of kids of colour being discriminated against. In stark contrast to what I have been told about similar schools during this period, it was certainly never grounds for bullying by other boys.

My mum's cousin and closest childhood confidante, Aunty Pat, married my uncle Dapo, a Nigerian medical student, in Sheffield in the 1960s and moved to Nigeria with him after graduation. We were such a small family unit growing up – Mum, Dad, me, my sister, three half-siblings on Dad's side who we barely saw and, for a short time, my granddad and a great-aunt – that our half-African cousins on the other side of the world were much more in my thoughts than they might otherwise have been. Any TV shows depicting the casual racism of the era seemed simply nonsensical to me because the black people I knew were so immeasurably far away from the stereotypes and clichés portrayed on screen.

They were much richer than us and would arrive in Kidderminster laden with the sort of presents we would normally only get at Christmas. One year, when we had been planning to make the trip to Nigeria to visit them – an almost unimaginable adventure for a boy who had never previously been further from Kidderminster than Blackpool – but some national emergency I can't now remember put paid to our plans. They instead invited us to stay with them in a suite of rooms at one of Knightsbridge's grandest hotels. Aged about six, I have two memories of the trip: there was, incredibly, a fridge that contained nothing but Pepsi and, until we were caught by our mums, my cousin Bode and I spent a very profitable afternoon going up and down in the lift charging Arab ladies a pound note to stroke my flaxen locks.

Even at big school, the very few boys of colour were generally from foreign royal families or simply very rich. There was a Hindu lad in my year, a supremely bright scholarship boy who, like me, was there more through parental sacrifice than parental wealth, and he ended up head of house. One of my closest friends was mixed race but it was never commented on except in the context of his insistence that we could never appreciate the importance of the hip hop group NWA in the way that he did. It is, obviously, very easy for me to say – and I know for a fact that this doesn't hold true for other fee-paying schools in the same era – but I don't think any of them were ever victimised for their ethnicity or colour. And we could be pretty brutal to each other.

At the London School of Economics, where I went to university, the mix was almost comically multicultural, though we were mostly fairly middle class. Years later, I found out – from a caller to my radio show – that a man who would regularly visit a Pakistani student who roomed next to me for six months went on to join Al-Qaeda and be convicted of terror offences, but my own circle was a veritable United Nations of ravers and lecture-skivers.

I explain all this in the hope of understanding how I could have ended up in my late twenties utterly and completely ignorant of how deeply entrenched base racism is at every single level of British society. My support for stop and search was a mere symptom of a much deeper ignorance.

My wife went out with a mixed-race man before we met and, after we had been together for a few months, she commented on how refreshing it was not to be stopped regularly by the police anymore as we drove around London. I genuinely didn't know what she was talking about. It turned out that her ex had driven a vintage sports car and would be routinely stopped by police and ordered to prove that it hadn't been stolen. Even then, I still argued that this was no big deal, that he could simply prove his ownership and be on his way. Nothing to hide, remember, nothing to fear. Besides, we were in a rubbish car and she did all the driving so it was hardly a valid comparison. I presume I just closed my ears to the frequency with which it had happened to her ex and, crucially, resisted any temptation to imagine how I would have felt in the same situation. It's a miracle she married me.

I'd like to think that I was somehow motivated by a reluctance to believe that my own country could harbour the sort of sentiments I associated with apartheid in South Africa and the Ku Klux Klan in America. I remember being taken on a National Front march by my dad in the very late seventies (he was covering it for his newspaper, not marching). He tried to explain to little me that some people just didn't like other people because of their skin colour but, again, that just sounded so silly. Oddly, I do have a memory of feeling sad about the fact that there were pushchairs and small children present, so I must have been aware on some level that this was a disgusting scenario but I would be lying if I said it had preyed on my mind. So while I'd *like* to think that I was somehow motivated by a reluctance to believe that my own country could harbour these sorts of sentiments, I don't in all conscience think that I can. I just didn't think about the issue and, worse, I never thought about the victims. I didn't notice any racism in my world and that was good enough for me. I don't know if you can ever break out of a mindset like that without help. Fortunately, the job I ended up doing has such help on tap.

One of the biggest myths surrounding the radio phone-in is that it is difficult to make the phones ring. It's incredibly easy. You just ask whether there's anybody old listening who's feeling poorly, or whether people have 'had enough of immigration', or if anyone out there has ever received a parking ticket that they think was undeserved. The challenge, for me, quickly became one of attracting *interesting* callers who would say things I had never heard before and even, perhaps, tell me things that would never have occurred to me because of the parameters of my own lived experience. On both sides of the Atlantic, stop and search is one of the hardiest phone-in perennials because everybody has an opinion. Especially in London, where my show was exclusively broadcast until going national in 2014.

At first, you're grateful for it. A thousand Bobs in Ongar or Dereks in Dorking, usually well into their sixties, miles away from the trouble spots and with no black acquaintances or personal experiences of stop and search whatsoever, are adamant that it's a welcome and necessary way of dealing with young, mostly black criminals. Most presenters would encourage, even echo, these sentiments and, for a while, I was one of them. I would, if pushed, argue sincerely that while support for indiscriminate stop and search was high among racists it was also perfectly possible to support it from a liberal and altruistic perspective. I think I believed that it was the best way to reduce the possibility of more young black boys being murdered.

It began to fall apart when I took to telling all the Bobs and Dereks listening that I didn't want them to ring me this time. Instead, I said that I wanted to hear only from people who had been stopped and searched by the police despite being guilty of no crime. Ideally, it would have happened to them more than once. As I've grown into the role, I've come to relish the challenge of setting the bar ever higher for callers on occasion, demanding proper knowledge of the subject in hand and, crucially, direct experience. But this was a bit of a gamble. Mercifully, it took about ten minutes for the phones to start ringing off the hook.

It is embarrassing to admit now that the first thing to shock me was the almost unanimous testimony about the *practice* of stop and search as opposed to the *principle*. It is a phone-in topic or an academic subject for most white people, not a fact of life. Pretty much every caller to whom it had happened had been left bruised by the experience and had felt victimised by the police. Not just by their attitude, which you could argue might be in the eye of the beholder, but by their words and actions. Before the advent of body cameras for police officers and, of course, camera phones for the general public it had clearly been commonplace for black men to be not just racially profiled (which I had somehow ended up being comfortable with) but also racially abused (which, obviously, I was not) by the police. I hesitate to say that this found me at my most naive because there is so much competition. But even after the 1999 Macpherson Report into the murder of Stephen Lawrence six years previously, which had described the Metropolitan Police as 'institutionally racist', I was staggered to learn how British police routinely spoke to black British people.

Calls to the show from that era have not survived but I believe that my position – borne out of that inability to admit to being wrong – was to insist that we were talking about the *principle* of stop and search and that we shouldn't get distracted by individual examples of police racism. The more calls we took the more my defence evolved into an argument that it was a perfectly acceptable policing tactic as long as the police behaved politely and respectfully. I clung on to this notion in various guises for much longer than I can justify.

A couple of years later, I used the same approach in order to speak to callers with experiences of knife crime. You could only come on air if you had actually carried a knife and could explain why. Again, a long queue of Bobs and Dereks formed to reminisce about pitched battles between mods and rockers in seaside towns in the sixties and explain how things were somehow different then. A good producer is adept at sorting wheat from chaff and soon we were again mining a rich seam of lived experience. One recurring theme took me by complete surprise. It had literally never occurred to me that the knife-carrying criminal I had been conditioned to fear might actually be frightened themselves. It quickly became clear that behaviour I had always taken as evidence of entrenched and deliberate criminality might be nothing of the sort. Andre is a perfect case in point.

James: So, Andre, you carried a knife?

Andre: For a bit, yeah.

James: How old are you now?

Andre: Twenty-five.

James: And how old were you when you first started carrying a knife around town.

Andre: Year eight, James, so about 13 or 14.

James: And why did you do it? Can you remember the first time you left the house with a knife secreted about your person? Had you bought it especially or had you just, I don't know, nicked it from the kitchen at home?

(Proper little Perry Mason, me.)

Andre: Yeah. It was my mum's knife. And I did it because I was scared.

James: Pardon?

Andre: I was scared. A kid from another school said he was going to stab me next time he saw me, so I thought I'd better get myself a knife.

James: Why?

Andre: Because if he was going to pull a knife on me then I had to have something to defend myself with, didn't I?

James: It doesn't sound like you were scared. It sounds like you were up for a fight.

Andre: What would you have done, James? This kid was nasty. He'd already hurt two of my friends, not with knives to be fair but he'd messed them up. And I honestly believed that he would stab me if he got the chance.

James: Couldn't you just have legged it if you saw him?

Andre: I did as it happens. A couple of times someone told me he was waiting for me outside school so I steered well clear.

James: But you still carried a knife?

Andre: Yeah, for about three months.

James: What happened then?

Andre: He stabbed someone else and got sent down.

It would be wrong to claim that this was one of those 'penny drop' moments for me. I would, back then, have expended enormous amounts of energy trying to persuade myself and my listeners that Andre's first-hand experience hadn't driven a coach and horses through my carefully cultivated support for stop and search. Support, I realise now, predicated upon a belief that publicly frisking innumerable innocent people was a price worth paying for the discovery of one person actually carrying a knife.

Why wasn't it obvious to me that fear would be a key component behind many young men's decision to arm themselves? In fact, much of the media coverage of 'knife crime' could almost be seen as encouragement to carry one if you live in the sections of the city most often affected. But it wasn't obvious because not only had I never experienced it, I'd never really thought about it. And that's the crucial point: the more I thought about it and the more I listened to people who had experienced this thing I had such strong opinions about, the harder it became to sustain those opinions. Weirdly, if I did something else for a living I think I might have been able to keep my position intact. I couldn't, though, because I not only relish listening to people with experiences a million miles away from my own, people utterly unqualified to enter my own 'echo chamber', but also interviewing prominent ones.

George the Poet is, as you probably know, a spoken-word artist whose work draws heavily on his own experiences growing up in the London suburb of Neasden. One of the most interesting people I've interviewed in recent years, he credits his avoidance of the crime and knife culture rife among his peers to a sense of self-worth distilled at home and, later, to the recognition at school of his considerable academic prowess. I was most interested when I last spoke to him by this question of what makes some boys reach for the knife in their family's kitchen drawer while other boys resist.

George the Poet: I was fast-tracked a year at primary school and I can't express what a confidence boost that is and how deeply that gives you a sense of advantage and a sense that things are going to work out from a young age. I always had that in the back of my mind. So when a lot of my friends, we all got into situations, various situations on their estate and in estate life and a lot of these situations sometimes would escalate into violence.

Sometimes someone was trying to save face. But as we got older, it became riskier and riskier. Knife crime became part of our youth. And I remember always feeling like it's never going to be that serious. I'm never going to have to, I'm never going to be so invested in my social life that I got to go and stab someone for my reputation. But some people don't see any other way. They don't feel any self-worth outside of their reputation among their social group, who they are. That's who they're becoming. And it doesn't occur to them that there's any other way.

Imagine going into a school where everyone knows that, for example, you just got robbed by someone else in your year and none of the girls are interested in you and everyone knows that you're an open. You're a target now because you got robbed once and you haven't got a defence and you don't have any olders. What are you going to do? Well, all of your parents' reasoning and your teachers' discipline isn't going to dissuade you from feeling like you got to go and take your name into your own hands.

James: I can't get over the idea of it being done by frightened people. The violence is supposed to be done by frightening people, not by frightened people, but what you describe is somebody who feels he has no options or he has no one to turn to ...

George: It's just your reality. That's how.

James: But *you* had options and you had the same reality so what was different?

George: Yeah, because I, because I was always told that I am an outstanding pupil. Oh, man. (laughs)

James: So with just a bit of encouragement, with a bit of evidence, you'd think, I can make it. Things could be different for me ...

George: Straight up. It's that simple. It is that simple, man. But it's like the encouragement needs to feel qualified. You know, you can't just come to someone and say, 'Hey, you could be everything that you want to be,' because you're going to say that to them and when you leave the room that idea disappears with you. Nothing about their environment tells them they can be everything they want to be, right? So thank you for your words, but that's where they are at this point. They're not going to manifest in any actual opportunity that's going to make them do anything differently. As much as I would love that.

I've always loved the Robert Frost poem 'The Road Not Taken'. When I suffered from pretty bad insomnia in the wake of my dad's death, long before I discovered the comforts of therapy, I used to try to memorise poems in the small hours in the hope of keeping the demons at bay. For the record, it was quite effective and the simple pleasure of committing poems to memory and then being able to retrieve them at will survived long after easy sleep returned. It was the famous final lines of Frost's poem that popped into my mind as George spoke.

Two roads diverged in a wood, and I—
I took the one less traveled by,
And that has made all the difference.

George: I'm not even going to lie, man. Things could have gone very differently. There were times. I remember my friend had a gun. I was about 14, 15. I've got a poem about this called 'Blame Game'. My friend had a gun we used to call a baby nine. And, um, he wanted to offload it. He wanted to sell it to someone and I just didn't have the money.

James: A proper Robert Frost moment. What if you had taken the other road? Why didn't you?

George: I just didn't have the money. If I had the money and I was able to, you know, if I was able to buy that gun, I would have had to think to myself about the risk of ending up in a violent altercation again when I'm unarmed. Versus knowing that as soon as they see *this*, there's no problem anymore. All my problems disappear. I go to a grammar school. What are they going to be like? There's no police around my school. I'm not going to be waving this thing around. But I've got an hour and a half journey to my school. I had to pass through so many different environments, different estates, different politics. Rest in peace, Kiyan Prince. He was a young man in my year group who was stabbed up at the age of 15.

Kiyan, who was murdered while trying to prevent the bullying of another boy, was, like George, black. The statistics beloved of right-wing blowhards are at least accurate. Knife crime is disproportionately committed – and suffered – by young black men and that, goes the argument, is why they should be treated differently from the rest of society. I fell for it because I never looked beyond the specific issue, and it took another writer of incredible talent to make me see the error of my ways.

A rapper, journalist, author, activist and poet from Kentish Town, Akala's seminal book, *Natives: Race and Class in the Ruins of Empire*, uses British history to effortlessly unpick the idea that 'knife crime' is somehow a 'black' problem. I know how arrogant this sounds but I'm going to say it anyway: I don't often feel intellectually intimidated and when I do I love it. For me, there is something so utterly infectious about the combination of raw intelligence, knowledge and passion for the subject matter that there are some people I could listen to all day. Akala would be very near the top of that list. Which is fortunate, as it's fair to say that when I last interviewed him, for once I struggled to get a word in edgeways. Thank goodness.

Akala's Scottish mother and Jamaican father separated before he was born and he was raised in what he has termed 'the clichéd, single-parent working-class family'. Exposed to 'gang' violence from an early age he carried a knife himself for a period. When we met in 2018, news of the so-called Windrush scandal had just broken in the British media, thanks largely to the work of the *Guardian* journalist Amelia Gentleman. The scandal concerned mostly British subjects of Caribbean origin who had been wrongly detained, denied legal rights, threatened with deportation and, in at least 83 cases, actually deported from the UK. All under the aegises of a Home Office committed to what the former home secretary, by now prime minister, Theresa May had described as a 'hostile environment' policy. Introduced in 2012, this was explicitly designed to make it as hard as possible for people without 'leave to remain' to stay in the UK in the hope that they would leave 'voluntarily'. It's clear to me now that if white people from, say, Tunbridge Wells had been treated similarly, the reverberations would likely have brought down May's government, but I began our interview by telling Akala that I found the idea of it all being part of a bigger, avowedly racist picture 'too sinister to believe'.

Akala: Which is understandable, given your lived experience. The first time I was searched by the police I was 12. There was no adult present, I wasn't read my rights. A teacher in my school had given all of us young black boys a form with our rights on it because he knew we were going to get searched by the police at some point. It doesn't matter what your grades are. Another time, I actually got searched on my way to the Royal Institution mathematics masterclasses and that was when it hit me – respectability politics don't mean anything.

James: (already reeling a bit) But what did they do to you?

Akala: Nothing. They just searched me.

James: But when you say that, I don't know what you mean. I've never been searched in my life ...

Akala: I was a very big lad so, in their defence, I didn't look 12 but I did try to explain. It was round the corner from my home in Kentish Town but the officer was like, 'Where are you from? Tottenham?' [At the time, Tottenham was notorious for gang-related violence.] So you know what he was trying to say from the jump, right? And the interesting thing is that I didn't tell my mum when I got home. I couldn't be bothered. I was just like, OK, cool. I knew this was coming because it's like a rite of passage so I thought, Meh, if I tell my mum she's going to get upset. She's going to feel like she needs to go to the police station and tell them this was wrong.

James: So back to respectability politics ...

Akala: I was born in the bottom 1 or 2 per cent socio-economically speaking but academically I was in the top 1 or 2 per cent. It didn't change the fact that some of the people with power saw a criminal. This was before I did become a bit of a naughty boy myself and part of that trajectory was being treated like a criminal. For me, at the kind of school I went to, I saw who was bringing drugs in to school and who wasn't. I saw who was getting searched and who wasn't and the kind of kids bringing drugs in to the school – class A drugs, anyway – were the kids that could afford it. There was weed, I'm not going to lie, but in terms of 'drugs' drugs, it wasn't us. So it was very clear to me very early, the lunacy of ethnically targeted stop and search which they want to bring back. When you look at the numbers now you see that it doesn't even help solve the problem. It helps make the problem worse for reasons that should be entirely common sense.

Let's say there's roughly a million black people in London – it's about 800,000, something like that. Let's say there's 40 or 50 murders a year. Say 50, just to make the maths easier. That means 5 in every 100,000 people or, to put it another way, 0.005 per cent of people actually kill somebody. I researched a lot of police reports from the days of Operation Trident [a Metropolitan Police unit set up in 1998 to tackle gun crime and homicide disproportionately affecting Afro-Caribbean communities] for my book and, you know, they understand very well that the type of young black boys that are likely to kill people are not random at all. When you adjust for abuse in the home, when you adjust for expulsion from school, crucially, you begin to see that they're the same socio-economic demographic as the kids who have been doing it in Glasgow or Liverpool, or Sheffield in the 1920s or Middlesbrough. But we can ignore all that so, ironically, treating the 85 or 90 per cent of young black boys in Hackney who just want to go to school and get a job like criminals actually prevents us from allocating the resources where they need to go, which is to help the most vulnerable. And the worst part about it is: if you're a kid like my little cousin, for example, and you live on a council estate in Hackney and you've been robbed two or three times growing up, you know boys have pulled a knife on you for your mobile phone, then you get searched by the police because of the very boys you're getting bullied by – of course you're going to be peed off. It's natural.

Let's put it like this. If we took the case of Jimmy Savile or Rolf Harris or whoever else and we said, 'Right, all middle-aged white guys in TV are potential paedophiles so let's police [all middle-aged white guys on TV] as if they might be paedophiles. When they go to pick up their grandkids let's stop them and make sure it is actually their grandkids because of what Jimmy Savile's done.' This is what you get when you get collective blame but we sort of accept it. And again, I don't even entirely blame the public because you have a language of public policy and you have a language of media that emphasises race whenever there's a negative story but not when there's a positive story.

The last time I got stopped was six months ago. It was literally a week after the Met commissioner went on TV and said 'tougher sentences for teenage thugs', 'black men in London are 20 times more likely to be killed', which is a very selective way of presenting the information. If you're saying blackness is the common denominator, the correct way to present the information would be to say what percentage of black people actually kill people. As I just showed you with the stats, you realise that it's significantly less than 1 per cent, which means you're going to have to offer more of a common denominator than blackness. When you present blackness as the common denominator – even when a significant proportion of the stats are made up of people like me who are half white – you get a situation where the police can pull over a grown man, 34 years old, and say 'gang members drive cars like this', and I'm like, 'Well, so do people who run companies. I'm actually on my way to a meeting. But thank you very much, I'm sure it was the car that made you think I was a gang member.'

The journalists who write the stuff about poor white kids doing badly at school are not concerned that poor white kids are failing, they're concerned that poor white kids are failing relative to black kids. They're not actually concerned with poor white kids themselves. There's a sort of weird racial nationalism that says we're OK for the chavs to fail but they shouldn't be failing more than the immigrants. And weirdly for me, who's done a lot of educational work in poor communities, I want all young kids to do well. I mean, why wouldn't we want more smart people?

I'd forgotten that line about smart people until I revisited the interview for this book. It's pretty haunting. Especially when you insert a politician or a newspaper proprietor or the anonymous funders of a 'think tank' dedicated to denigrating immigrants or seeking tax cuts for the already absurdly wealthy. Why wouldn't *they* want more smart people? The question quickly becomes rhetorical, right?

As I write, America is literally on fire. In May 2020, a Minneapolis police officer was filmed kneeling on the neck of a black man, George Floyd, for 8 minutes and 46 seconds as the life seeped out of his 46-year-old body. Within hours of the footage going live, protests and later riots across the country assumed a terrifying urgency and scale. Police officers arrested Omar Jimenez, a black CNN journalist, live on air for no apparent reason and fired shots – again, on camera – at other reporters. Donald Trump, who had spent his presidency stoking hatred of a free media, offering sympathy and support to white armed militias *storming government buildings* and doubling down on the white supremacist bile that had seen him embrace the ridiculous 'birther' movement surrounding Barack Obama's origins, tweeted a call for 'looters' to be shot and was, unprecedentedly, cautioned by Twitter for 'glorifying violence'.

Watching on TV, I found myself – between bouts of despair at what might unfold – wondering how anyone honest could still deny the racism so obviously endemic in American society. And by recalling my own blindness to British equivalents I tried to formulate some answers. Certainly, some people simply do not want to believe that they live in a racist society. It would not be helpful to castigate them for their innocence. But there comes a point where that innocence segues into a wilful ignorance – a refusal rather than a failure to acknowledge the evidence. These people are the ones who ring me most angrily and yet I still find it very difficult to condemn them out of hand. I suffer from a conviction that if you hit people too hard with accusations of racism and bigotry, you run a very real risk of pushing them further into their prejudices.

Looking at the scenes in America today, however, I fear this sounds like surrender.

I failed to appreciate the insidiousness of ethnically targeted stop and search – and the broader problem it highlights – but if I had clung to my position *after hearing the evidence* I think I would have become dishonest, even dangerous. I used to laugh along with colleagues who, when presented with undeniable evidence that their on-air arguments were bogus, would comically put their fingers in their ears and sing, 'La, la, la.' I don't laugh now. Especially not in the arena of racism. Especially now that I have been compelled, by the vagaries of the British media, to work alongside actual and unapologetic racists.

It would have staggered six-year-old me, giggling in a Knightsbridge lift with my half-Nigerian cousin as we relieved Arab ladies of their pound notes, but my country, my home, is full of people who would have judged us according to our skin colour. The difference between a history of slavery and a history of colonialism (or empire) is such that there are profound differences between the scale and nature of racism in America and Britain today. But the single, unifying truth is that it is real and it is pretty much everywhere. And if it's pretty much everywhere then it will, indubitably, be well-represented in media and politics. So the columnists who hint that one unsubstantiated allegation somehow undermines a thousand proven ones, the broadcasters who talk glibly about 'the race card' being played and the tweeters and phone-in callers who bridle and baulk at the mention of 'white privilege' are all complicit, all culpable. The politicians who talk about 'low-skilled' immigrants and vow to 'keep them out' are not addressing 'legitimate concerns' but appealing to ancient hatreds that persist mostly because they protect power, privilege and wealth from the forces of equality, decency and justice. Post-9/11, the largely successful attempts by precisely these journalists and politicians to render all Muslims somehow suspicious quickly bled into their treatment of other minorities. This was no accident. It allowed a resurgence in the sort of language and opinion that, in the years since I saw those pushchairs at that National Front march, had been largely neutered by the march of common decency and liberal values. Of course, the columnists and commentators unduly and incessantly exercised by, for example, left-wing black female politicians still call the forces of fundamental fairness 'political correctness'.

I don't know how to fight it. I don't think there is an even vaguely popular platform in the British media that doesn't routinely promote and amplify the sort of reality-denying 'opinions' that we are still shy of accurately describing as base racism. The effort put into ridiculing the very word, never mind the practice, infects the very highest levels of our society, and while I do believe that some of the people who still deny its ubiquity can genuinely still not see it, there are plenty who clearly can. They know exactly what they are doing and the rest of us let them. Cowed by the social-media pile-ons or the newspaper hatchet jobs or, perhaps, by our own impotence, we all risk unconsciously indulging Donald Trump's sick suggestion that there are 'some very fine people on both sides' – even when the people on one side are basically Nazis.

My own answer, for now, is to prescribe the treatment that worked for me: facts, evidence, other people's lived experiences. Look, listen, learn and then strain to help other people do the same. It may not be enough. If it isn't, there will be more George Floyds dying on our screens and more black British people filming British police treating them in a way that nobody white will ever experience. I know it's not enough but it is, for now, all I've got.

The British journalist and author Sathnam Sanghera, whose book *The Boy with the Topknot* tells the tale of his Sikh family in seventies Wolverhampton, expressed this inadequacy perfectly in a tweet he posted in the midst of the George Floyd protests:

> *A brutal truth about the media: the only time black people are given a sustained hearing is at times like this, when they are pleading to be treated with basic human dignity. It has been an industry failure for as long as I have been in it and it fucking breaks my heart.*

If you feel yourself resisting these statements, I get it. I did too. It sometimes seems that the mountain is so high it would be easier never to start climbing and even to pretend that it isn't really there. But it is. You know that it is. We all do.

Why is stop and search the lens through which I find it easiest to see all of this? Partly because it is such a flashpoint of race relations, partly because I so effortlessly ended up being so wrong about it and partly because it makes it impossible for honest people to ignore that mountain.

The Canadian journalist and author Malcolm Gladwell often, like Akala, left me reeling in his cerebral wake when he opened up some of this thinking for me in 2019 while discussing his book *Talking to Strangers*. His work has long explored stop and search policies. He provides a view from the other side of the thin blue line, conscious always that the priority of community policing should be the community. When stop and search is examined in the British media, it is invariably framed as a stand-off between police and *all* young black men. This framing completely, and often deliberately, ignores the fact that pretty much everybody in the communities most affected would rather things were different. Sadly, it often seems that the priorities of people living with the daily reality of crime are ignored while police and politicians instead address the sensibilities of people in leafy suburbia living lives untouched by the scourges of casual violence and illegal drugs. People like me. It is impossible to see how any meaningful progress can be made while the targeting of innocent members of the communities most affected persists. If the white sons of the most reactionary and racist columnists and politicians in the country were routinely stopped by often aggressive police and ordered to prove their innocence of various unspecified offences, the practice would be abandoned by teatime.

Gladwell: I spent an afternoon when I was reporting my book driving around Baltimore, one of the most dangerous cities in the West, with a researcher who was part of this whole movement to understand the connection between place and crime. We drove through all of the worst areas of Baltimore and she would ask me periodically every two minutes, 'Do you think this block is dangerous?' And I would, you know. It would be run down. There would be people loitering the streets. And the point was that most of the places that look dangerous have virtually no crime. She would say, 'This particular block had 150 police calls last year. The next block over had 2.' So she says, 'On this block, flooding it with police officers is perfectly legitimate but if you do it on the next block over you are harassing perfectly innocent people and they will resent you for it. But if you focus the police on the block with 150 calls last year, they will welcome you there because these are people who are imprisoned in their homes.'

And the other thing is it doesn't move. So one idea is that if you just crack down on one block they'll move one block over. It turns out not to be true. Crime is rooted to place. It moves very slowly and kind of grudgingly.

If you overlay crime onto a map of London, you will see this precise phenomenon. There are very small sections of London that are responsible for overwhelming numbers of the crime. What that means is if you're going to use aggressive, proactive policing, it is entirely appropriate in those 2 per cent of neighbourhoods where crime is endemic. It is not appropriate anywhere else. Right. We've operated on the assumption that if there is lots of crime in the city, it means that police need to be everywhere and be aggressive all the time. No, no. Completely wrong lesson. You need to be incredibly cautious, strategic and tactical in the way you use police power.

I already had this book in mind when I met Malcolm so I also asked him the question at its heart.

James: How do you process being wrong?

Gladwell: I actually quite like being wrong. First of all, I think it's evidence that I'm human. Also, there's something terribly unattractive about people who won't change their mind. I like to be around people who will kind of say, 'Oh!' and revisit what they were. And the process of revisiting what you used to believe is in some sense sort of exhilarating. But it's also weirdly a way, I feel, like it's a way of remaining young, of maintaining a sense of being surprised.

> So I welcome that ... If someone wants to, you know, take one part of my book and say, 'You got it all wrong. Here's why,' show me your work and I will quite happily switch sides tomorrow.
>
> **James:** I know you've suggested that you put too much emphasis on the broken window theories of policing right at the beginning of your career ...

The 'broken windows' theory of policing was first described in a 1982 article by social scientists James Q. Wilson and George L. Kelling. Essentially, it argued that low level crime leads to high level crime and so clamping down on offences like vandalism, public drinking and fare evasion would see a reduction in more serious offences. In the 1990s, the policing policies of New York City Police Commissioner William Bratton and Mayor Rudy Giuliani were heavily influenced by the theory. It was seen by them as a justification for widespread stop and frisking.

> **Gladwell:** I've been writing about crime obsessively for about 20 years now. And my understanding today and the understanding of the criminological community is so different from my understanding of 20 years ago when I began.
>
> **James:** Can you give a couple of examples?

Gladwell: Well, for example, this notion of crime being tightly coupled to place is a very new idea. It's a ten-year-old idea. Had I known, had any of us known that 20 years ago, we would have tackled the crime waves of the 1990s in a very different manner and with far less social consequences. I mean, I think the kind of backlash against the police that we've seen here as well as in America in recent years is a function of not knowing that crime was something that was so specific to certain particular problematic areas. That would be crucial. I think, like many people, I underestimated the power of numbers in policing. That really makes a difference, how many police officers you have. And that was not something that was well understood in the 1990s. I think I have more and more become convinced of the futility of imprisonment. I would not have said that 20 years ago. Now, there are very, very few people, I think, who belong in prison. I really think the institution is just stupid and barbaric, but that's, again, something that's emerged relatively recently.

He certainly made me feel a bit better about my own errors of judgment but the real challenge, it seems to me, is to get such thoughts and insights in front of people who, unlike Gladwell, really don't like being wrong and rarely, if ever, admit it. It's why I do relish time spent with such people. They seem in many ways to be the key to unlocking the sort of stagnation and stubbornness that led to America and the United Kingdom being led by Donald Trump and Boris

Johnson – both averse to detail but provenly fond of stoking bigotries and division in pursuit of power – even as we faced a global pandemic of unprecedented power and proportion. At the time of writing, they are vying for the title of world leader who handled the outbreak worst, but their so-called 'bases' of support remain largely unmoved, even as the death tolls mount.

I think I was lucky, by the way. I think I arrived in the job at a time in my life when I was still able, even keen, to review my opinions. With a background in showbusiness journalism, I hadn't actually spent much time thinking about the 'big' stuff that we're required to serve up most days on the radio. If I'd come from a newspaper where lazy and provocative 'othering' was editorial policy, where readers were encouraged to be fearful and suspicious of anybody who looks 'different' from them, it's perfectly possible that I would have been too far down the rabbit hole of institutionalised racism ever to climb out. Similarly, if I'd had bosses that valued quantity of calls above quality – a very easy thing to do in this market – I would have stayed in my lane and spoken to countless Bobs and Dereks about things that neither of us knew anything about.

I'm not under any illusions about my own road not taken, either. All I ever wanted to do was follow my dad into newspaper journalism, and if the career fairy hadn't waved her wand when she did it's more than likely I would have ended up writing – or at least writing alongside – the sort of stuff that disgusts me so deeply today. I hope I wouldn't have been among the worst offenders but if it was a proven recipe for success, and I turned out to have a gift for it, I think I might have followed it. I know I would have published it if refusing to do so would have halted my own ascent up the greasy pole. It seems important to admit this. I'm not holier than thou, just luckier.

Chapter 4
WHITE PRIVILEGE, BLACK LIVES

I FINISHED THE LAST chapter and patted myself on the back for being such a clear-eyed ally of Black Lives Matter. Then I went to work, started a phone-in asking how on earth decent people end up in a place where they can't see any racism in the killing of George Floyd and promptly made an absolute fool of myself.

Before I don the hair-shirt, I should probably clarify a few things. I am supremely unconvinced that anybody genuinely needs help understanding what support for the Black Lives Matter movement really means. However, so many people in and out of the public eye profess not to understand that it might be worthwhile to take their confusion at face value. A belief in the importance of those three words does not, obviously, entail a subscription to or belief in everything espoused by any formal organisation that has those three words in its title. The unseemly desperation with which many consciously and subconsciously racist commentators sought to conflate support for basic human equality with support for everything from the collapse of capitalism to the abolition of the police was – as with so much of the far right rhetoric – simultaneously seductive and ridiculous. Similarly, the retort of 'All Lives Matter' is also of course duplicitous to the point of absurdity. Black Lives Matter is already a call for 'all lives' to 'matter' as much as each other – because currently they clearly don't.

The deliberate disingenuousness of 'All Lives Matter' in this context reminds me of a uniquely chilling moment in George Orwell's *Animal Farm* when the ruling class of pigs, in order to both normalise *and* deny their own epic privilege, start insisting that, 'All animals are equal, but some animals are more equal than others.' I can't currently get a cigarette paper between this infamous dictate and the insistence that 'All Lives Matter' (But Some Lives Matter More Than Others …). I doubt anyone acting in good faith can, to be honest, but people not yet prepared to declare publicly that they believe skin colour *should* determine a citizen's treatment in society are fond of using the phrase to obfuscate the reality of their prejudice.

Working once again on the probably false premise that this stuff actually *needs* explaining, the BLM movement's mission is, very simply, to create societies in which a citizen's treatment at the hands of the police, employers, the education system or simply the wider public will not be in any way determined by the colour of their skin. I say 'very simply', but when you try to apply what seems obvious in theory to the lived experiences of millions of different people, things get a little trickier. The phrase 'white privilege' is most illustrative of the problem.

It would be bold to say the least to look a white man in the eye and tell him he enjoys unfair and unjustified 'privilege' when he can see no evidence of it in his own life and, moreover, when he is profoundly unhappy with the state of it. When someone who feels that they do not have as much money, status, power or success as they deserve is told, often aggressively and accusatorially, that they are actually the beneficiaries of unearned privilege, they do not have to be in the foothills of the Ku Klux Klan to take umbrage. And it then does not take much effort for someone to take that umbrage and, with weasel words and provocations, turn it into a belief that 'they' get help and support while 'we' do not. You can even see, when using the lens of 'white privilege' to examine the bigger picture, how easy it would be to sow the seeds of the idea that because nobody is marching or protesting or agitating for *you*, then *you* are the real victim of discrimination. It culminates, inevitably, in cerebrally challenged but breathtakingly entitled public-school-educated white men being paid to opine in television studios and magazine columns that the phrase 'white privilege' is itself racist! (I hardly ever use exclamation marks but very occasionally no other punctuation will suffice.) I don't have the answer to this problem but I do know that we can't come close to solving it while these people continue not only to make these ludicrous claims, but also to shroud themselves in bogus victimhood when they are challenged.

To call for someone to stop spouting such divisive and demonstrably ridiculous bilge in the public space is, in the parlance of modern media martyrdom, to call for them to be 'cancelled'. Meanwhile, to simply see and describe the reality of discrimination, most obviously through racism, misogyny and homophobia, is to be 'woke'. To insist that these ghouls at least back up their rhetoric with a scintilla of reason or explanation is, again, to threaten their 'freedom of speech'.

Explaining all this is a mission as important as it is exhausting, but to see it euphemistically described as one side of a 'culture war' in the UK and USA just as right-wing governments led by men accused of serial race-baiting presided over two of the most inept and lethal responses to the Covid-19 pandemic on the planet was, to say the least, frustrating. This may seem like quite a leap but if politicians are propelled to power on a promise to hurt one section of society, while pledging to address the imagined or exaggerated grievances of another, everybody loses. Think of it as a toolbox. You can win elections and referendums with one that only contains the rusty spanners of xenophobia and othering but you can't do much else, least of all cope with massive and unforeseen challenges. The penny really dropped for me when Crystal Minton, a Trump supporter frustrated by the impact of America's belated and inadequate Covid-19 lockdown, told the *New York Times* in June 2020: 'I voted for him, and he's the one who's doing this. I thought he was going to do good things. He's not hurting the people he needs to be hurting.'

That last line unlocks everything. It explains how Trump supporters can be reduced to cheering him for drinking a glass of water even as the country's Covid death toll rocketed sky-wards. The demagogue who promises to hurt your enemies demands not to be judged on how his actions and policies impact on his supporters, only by how much he hurts their foes. An even starker and arguably more depressing example emerged on this side of the Atlantic in August 2020. Shortly after her government was found to have presided over both the second highest excess death rate in Europe and the deep-est recession in the G7, the home secretary, Priti Patel, report-edly boasted that her new immigration policies would 'send the left into meltdown'. Contrast this with what German Chancellor Angela Merkel explained in a speech to the Euro-pean Parliament on 8 June 2020: 'We are seeing at the moment that the pandemic can't be fought with lies and disinforma-tion, and neither can it be with hatred and agitation.' I warned in my last book of the dangers that lay ahead if we left the lies, othering and scaremongering behind the triumphs of Trump and Brexit unpunished but I didn't envision anything like the death tolls from a global pandemic in our two countries dwarf-ing almost every other. And while Merkel's conclusion that 'fact-denying populism is being shown its limits' may seem obvious to many of us, there are none so blind as those that will not see.

There are none so blind as those that will not see. Like me, when Emma in Kensal Rise rang my show in the immediate aftermath of George Floyd's killing in response to the question, what do white people most need help understanding about systemic racism? I didn't think I meant *white people like me*, but it turned out I was wrong.

What made the following lesson particularly painful for me was the way in which it highlighted how, despite the conversation I'd had with Akala a year or two previously, I still hadn't noticed how profoundly class had framed some of my own attitudes to race. When I'd railed against racism in the past, I think I held in my head the idea that the victims were somehow from worlds entirely different from my own. It is, perhaps, why calls from men of colour who had been in gangs or simply struggled with dysfunction or disadvantages had failed to reach parts of me that Emma, whose social class and status are outwardly much more similar to my own, zoned in on almost immediately.

Emma: Hi, James, and thanks for having me on. We spoke a while back about the BAFTAs. I'm a screenwriter of colour.

James: I remember.

Emma: Thank you. I'm sorry. I'm very angry at the moment. So please excuse me but I just feel like one of the basic tenets of this conversation is about the representation of black people and people of colour on our screen. And if we do not pass the microphone to people of a different ethnicity, of a different cultural background, of a different colour of skin – who happen to be British or happen to be American – and humanise them, then we will never, ever get past the fact that people are 'others'. I'm thinking about the fact that – and this is something I notice because I'm from East Asian heritage – very recently with the coronavirus, every single article that you saw in the beginning had an accompanying picture of an East Asian or Chinese person, usually wearing a mask. So all you do is you spread the idea that people from China are coronavirus carriers – and we've had a huge amount of corona racism towards Chinese and East Asian people in this country because of it – when actually the truth is that the coronavirus got spread over here by a white guy who went to, I think it was Singapore then Italy and became a super spreader. So for me, because obviously I'm a writer, it matters so much.

I'm afraid I became a little irritated here. Incredibly, given that this is a book in large part about how my uniquely personal perspective on the world was almost entirely framed by my own life and times, I balked at Emma's second mention of her writing career or, when you think about it, her status. I felt, in that moment, that a conversation about a black American victim of police brutality had nothing to do with her career or status. I was telling her, effectively, that her lived experience was not relevant having explicitly promised her that, as a woman of colour, I wanted to hear it. Her line about passing the microphone had, I realise now, hit me rather hard. It made me culpable, triggered an echo of the survival personality and put me, as we'll see, immediately and inappropriately on the defensive. And when put on the defensive, the old me immediately goes on the offensive. It's outrageous, really, but it's the best explanation I've got: for all my carefully burnished liberal credentials and the outward sincerity of my original phone-in question, when it came to systemic racism this white man still saw himself as a teacher not a pupil, still less an actual participant. The weirdest thing is that I show in my next reply to Emma that I did sort of grasp that this is a problem, but I couldn't, for some reason, follow through on the thought.

Emma: Trying to get stories, our stories from the people who our stories actually belong to, onto the screen or onto the radio is nigh on impossible because the gatekeepers who generally are editing and making, you know, making the decisions about who gets on are white.

James: They're not just white but, to use myself as an example, they're generally white people who congratulate themselves daily on their liberalism while clearly contributing unconsciously to the problem that you described. So, you know, guilty as charged *up to a point*, but what could be done differently?

Emma: Well, OK. OK, I'm going to say something really uncomfortable for you, James, and I thought a long time about this. I listen to you every day. I listen to your station and I really like the presenters that you have on but there is only one person of colour as a presenter on the whole station. And there is only one woman who is a full-time presenter.

James: The defence of that is – and I can't argue with you, you're stating facts. Everybody that listens knows that what you describe is simply true. But the defence, of course, is that, and this will sound flimsy to you, but there are people who could work here but have elected not to. And similarly, there are commercial imperatives. You know, this is a station on which if you don't deliver the numbers, you don't hang around, and they can't experiment. I'm not defending. I'm just explaining. I walk the tightrope every day between excusing and explaining. And I'd probably put in a third point here, which would be I don't think that having more presenters of colour or more women on the schedule at LBC would have helped keep George Floyd alive. And I would just cautiously steer you back to the conversation that we're having. I understand your grievance, you've explained it very well. But I want you to tell me about white people who see racism and somehow persuade themselves that they don't because that is – at risk of endorsing the patriarchy, Emma – that is the conversation that we are having on this programme today.

There's a smile in my voice when I deliver that line about endorsing the patriarchy but I cringe when I listen back to it. Read my response again. Could it be any more patronising?

Could it be any clearer that I am telling a woman of colour who has called in to tell me, a white man, about elements of racism that I, as a white person, may not understand to get back in her lane. Not even *her* lane, to be scrupulous, but the lane I want to confine her to. I don't know whether this makes things better or worse but, though I didn't know it at the time, it's pretty clear with the benefit of hindsight that her truths were becoming uncomfortable and I wanted to close her down. So I did. And the power bestowed by my privilege – whether by dint of my ethnicity, my gender, my status, my class or the dynamics of my radio show – allowed me to. Seriously, I'm wincing at this as I write and it happened years *after* we proudly stuck the *New Statesman*'s description of me as the 'conscience of liberal Britain' on the cover of my last book.

Emma: OK, James, I hear you. And I will, OK. I'll go back in the direction you want. But to answer that question fully – the question about people who see racism but don't think they do – then how do I do that if you call out something that is coming from me? I mean, you've just talked to me about your radio station and the business imperative . . .

James: But I want to talk about George Floyd.

Emma: Yes. So, OK.

James: He's never heard of James O'Brien or this radio station or any of my colleagues. This is a conversation about systemic racism in America that has seen a man die with a knee on his neck and now, I mean, again, you raise valid points, but I am talking about rather bigger issues than representation in the media.

Emma: Why? I mean ... Why is it ...

James: On a radio station in London, Emma.

Emma: But I would replicate everything that you say about a radio station in London, in England, to media across Western countries like the USA and like the UK, and how women and women of colour and people of colour are portrayed on screen ...

I *think* part of my problem here is that I hear her airing personal grievances as opposed to providing evidence of systemic discrimination. It's no excuse but it is at least an explanation. It's also, for a presenter who regularly preens himself for preferring 'experience' to mere 'opinion', spectacularly hypocritical.

James: I just want one last go. So here's the question: how does that help? As I sit here describing and detailing racism on an almost daily basis, how does the diversity of a radio station's line-up help people to a place where they're lying to themselves about racism? That's all I'm interested in this hour.

Emma: OK. How does the penny drop for somebody who thinks that they're not racist but doesn't contribute to a conversation about racism because they think that they are not racist, but they don't understand what racism is?

James: (very smugly) Well, you've lost me now. Which is probably my fault. But I just, I think perhaps it's not, it's not the day for the discussion that you want to have. I'm more interested in a) the deaths in America, and b) in the blatant racism of Donald Trump as opposed to the programming choices on this radio station, and c) in the co-opting of Christianity last night in a way that I find unprecedented and deeply, deeply frightening. [Trump had been photographed holding a Bible in front of a church in a square that had been cleared of peaceful BLM protesters by security guards using tear gas.] So perhaps in the foothills of this journey, some of the things that you described should and would be addressed and I am fully conscious of the enormous privilege that I have in being able to say this to you on a very popular radio programme, but again, you know, if you want to talk about the presenter line-up here, then drop a line to the programme controller. Because I've got a switchboard full of people who want to talk about George Floyd's death, Emma.

Emma: Of course. I completely understand. And I didn't want to attack you …

James: (painfully condescending now) I know you didn't. And I've taken on board a lot of what you said. And I'm uncomfortable pointing it out to you but that is what we are here for today and that is what we will continue to do after the news ...

And just like that, she's gone. Sledgehammered off the switchboard by my despicable suggestion that by being thoughtful and informed and drawing on her lived experience as a woman of colour, she was somehow seeking to distract from the death of George Floyd. Why did I do it? Clearly, I see now, because what she was saying strayed a little too close to home. This, in a way, was me baulking at the notion of 'white privilege' in my own life.

I spent years worrying that I wasn't getting any of the life prizes I considered my due. A strong marriage and happy family not-withstanding, I just didn't feel that my status as a little-known phone-in host, TV pundit and occasional newspaper columnist was befitting of my skills and talents. I turned 40 in 2012 convinced that my career had peaked and I was, quite frankly, gutted. More, I would worry desperately about losing what I did have, lying in bed at night calculating what would happen to our financial situation if the radio station replaced me with someone 'famous' and being rewarded with bouts of buzzing insomnia.

When my father passed away at the end of that year, I real-ised as I sorted through his effects that he'd seen his job as such an intrinsic part of his identity that when his journalism career ground to a halt, largely against his will, something inside him broke that could never be fixed. The realisation changed everything for me. My hero, the man whom I had only ever wanted to emulate as father, husband and journalist, had, it seemed to me, completely missed what mattered most in life and tortured himself with the loss of what didn't. And all the stuff that didn't matter was, of course, the self-same stuff that was keeping me awake at night.

In contrast to my late dad, I wanted to abandon the conviction that my value as a man somehow depended upon my professional status and success. I miss him most when I think about this because there is always this nagging, ridiculous thought that if I'd spent more time telling him that his value to us had absolutely nothing to do with his national newspaper bylines or his award nominations or his carefully preserved plaudits from the legendary *Daily Telegraph* editor Bill Deedes, then he might somehow still be with us. So I started moving, slowly and tentatively, towards the belief that those 'life prizes' were nowhere near as important as I had always believed.

I'm not remotely embarrassed to tell you that prayer played a large part in this process for me. The process doesn't *need* to be remotely religious – and, of course, I learned a few years later that therapy can sometimes play this role even more effectively than prayer for some people – but this move away from fretting over things you can't control towards working on the things you can was the first step towards achieving a sense of emotional security that I would not have believed possible when Dad died. Happily, and probably not coincidentally, the more I moved away from the notion that life is defined by 'prizes', the more the prizes that I'd thought were beyond my reach started landing in my lap.

I mention all of this because when I tried to work out why I had reacted unreasonably at Emma's words, I realised that I really had subconsciously bought into my own version of the idea that 'white privilege' had nothing to do with me. Because I had spent years mourning the absence of things that I believed somehow due to me – status, success, security – but that I thought I would never have, I bridled at the notion that achieving them was, even in part, down to my skin colour as opposed to the epic effort I felt I had put into understanding myself and my place in the world. How dare you call us privileged, the thought process goes, when in our secret hearts white men like my dad and me consider ourselves to have 'failed'? Or, simpler still: how dare you claim that we had a head start in a race we didn't win?

Emma was very clearly describing a head start enjoyed at different levels by all Western white people. We see ourselves reflected in the world around us in a way that non-white people simply do not. We may still have enormous mountains to climb to get to where we think we want to be in life but we are born varying degrees higher up the slopes than people of colour. So it is that the notion of 'white privilege' sticks in the craw of people looking only at the mountains' peaks and never over their shoulders at the people who started the climb behind them.

Of course, if one of those people should actually overtake us, if a person of colour should scale the highest heights, then that can be quickly turned into a bogus but seductive argument that there is no such thing as white privilege. For example, in history books of the future it will be impossible to explain the election of Donald Trump without reference to the undiagnosed psychic damage visited upon millions of white Americans by the election of Barack Obama eight years previously.

Here's a rather less profound illustration of the problem as it manifested in my own life. One of those prizes that landed in my lap *after* I had stopped worrying incessantly about my failure to win any of them was the opportunity to present television programmes for the BBC. It didn't last. As I've explained, long before various fraudsters and charlatans started bleating about 'cancel culture' in an attempt to avoid justifying their own bigoted rhetoric, I was compelled to step down from the corporation because of my now proven convictions about the depravity of Donald Trump and the impossibility of Brexit delivering any of the benefits promised by its cheerleaders. But it was great while it lasted, particularly when I got to sit in the driving seat of the flagship current affairs discussion show, *Newsnight*.

Not long after I started occasionally presenting it, I remember, with complete clarity, an exchange during the production meeting that, because of my background on newspapers and commercial radio, I thought at first was a joke. Researchers had assembled a three-person panel of various luminaries to discuss some now forgotten issue of the day, and the (very talented) editor of the programme insisted that we needed to change the panel line-up because it consisted entirely of oldish white men.

In every other corner of my career I would have sniggered out loud at this suggestion. Perhaps more significantly, I would have presumed that I was supposed to. I had done radio phone-ins about how jobs should always go to the 'best-qualified' candidate, apparently without noting that it could hardly be a coincidence that they almost always turned out to be white. I had been absolutely furious when, during a particularly fallow period in my own working life, a famous female friend had greeted the news that I was up for a juicy job with the line: 'Oh, that's just what we need, another posh, straight white man on the telly.' And then, when the pilot programme we made failed to cut the mustard, the message came back from the commissioning editor that, 'We loved James, but do you think you can find him in black?'

Subconsciously, all of this had conspired in my mind to create a very real sense that I had somehow *overcome* problems born of my own skin colour. So, for all my noble tub-thumping about other people's blindness to racism and white privilege, Emma poked a sore point I didn't know I had when she introduced the notion that I wouldn't have been on the radio if I hadn't been white. It's funny, because I positively proselytise about the facts that I wouldn't be on the radio or the TV or writing this book if I hadn't been adopted by the best parents or given an expensive education and its attendant 'access all areas' laminated passes, but the idea that I had also benefited from being white was a step too far. It's not hard to see why. My education was a gift from my parents. Their sacrifice and effort singled me out. Advantages accrued by my skin colour cannot be cast in such a noble light and so it was more comforting to deny that they existed at all.

Of course, I didn't work all this out in the immediate aftermath of binning Emma's call to the radio show. I did, however, read hundreds of mostly polite and measured tweets, texts and emails castigating me while we were still on air in the strongest terms for behaving so poorly. Pre-therapy, I would doubtless have doubled down on the offence, insisting that *you* don't know how the industry works, and perhaps even reached for the latest word-weapons of the terminally wrong and called my critics 'woke' or 'snowflakes'. Alternatively, perhaps I would have closed my eyes, put my fingers in my ears and pretended that the whole thing had never happened. I might even have railed against the 'mob' trying to close down my 'freedom of speech' because that is a lot easier than thinking, reflecting and admitting mistakes. Post-therapy, though, I take those highly adrenalised feelings of fear and persecution and, instead of transforming them into aggression or arrogance, I ask myself whether I am, actually, in the wrong.

Ultimately, you can only ever trust your own moral compass with this question, regardless of how vituperative or supportive online commentary might be, and on this occasion my compass was pointing squarely at 'wrong'. So I did something I don't think I've ever done before on the radio. I rang the caller back some two hours later to apologise and make amends.

James: Before we go on, I've been looking at the criticism I've received for the way I spoke to Emma earlier. Emma rang in to talk about why what you'd call systemic racism so often goes unrecognised and I can't lie to you, I think most of it is actually fair and accurate. I think that the criticisms you've sent to me, if I were to ignore them, it would make me a hypocrite. And so I think the only thing I can do to make amends is to invite Emma back onto the programme and do my very best not to interrupt her as she makes the points that she sought to make when we spoke a couple of hours ago. Emma is in Kensal Rise. Emma, what would you like to say?

Emma: (referring to the online brouhaha we – well, I – had prompted) Hi. Sorry, I'm feeling a bit nervous because it's been quite a manic morning. And I'm so, thank you, so much for having me back on. I think the truth is these kinds of conversations when you want to talk about racism are incredibly uncomfortable. Because what happened to George Floyd? What I was trying to very unclearly say before is ...

James: (clearly struggling to articulate myself) No, the fault was mine. Please don't. Don't, don't, don't apologise. It was my fault. I didn't hear everything you said and I responded wrongly to what you did say. So don't, don't say that you did anything wrong. That was my bad entirely.

Emma: OK, James. Thank you. What happened to George Floyd is symptomatic of how people of colour, black people – and there is a spectrum of people of colour as well – how we are portrayed in our cultural narratives. And I think we cannot distance ourselves from the fact that the power of the narratives that we are told on our TV screens and on our radio stations and on social media now too is almost primarily controlled by white gatekeepers. And that is about holding power. And you talk a lot about the non-dom billionaires who own the papers that most people in this country read. And they pay for and decide the narratives about all the other things that you discuss in your shows all the time. And probably the biggest problem that we have, in terms of how to overcome racism, even for people who want to do the right thing, is that the truth is when you have power, you don't want to let it go. And in the media, in my industry, the truth is that it is a competitive industry and becoming a popular radio presenter like you takes years and it also takes talent but it also takes a gate that is open to you that is shut to a lot of other people. And part of the reason for it being shut to them is how they look and how they speak and backgrounds that don't align with what the gatekeepers think is what they want to hear or what they want to broadcast, but also what they themselves are interested in. That's why we don't have any drama shows on TV generally that are predominantly casting people of colour. And when we do they are portrayed as stereotypes. So people who are Muslim are generally portrayed as people who are terrorists. East Asian people are triads or, for women, docile, quiet or, you know, prostitutes. I mean, that is the stereotyping that goes on that fits the narrative of what our audiences or at least the gatekeepers think our audiences want to see. And until we challenge that, and until we turn that around, we can't truly get people to look at people of colour, and people of different ethnicities, and see somebody who is fully human. And the really uncomfortable point about this, James, is that it means that white people who are privileged have to give up their platform. And when I talked about your station – and I know this is difficult so I can talk about any other broadcaster ...

James: No, you can say whatever you want, Emma. Absolutely whatever you want.

Emma: OK. Why is there only one woman and one person of colour on your station? Look at the line-up and it is almost all white males of a certain age.

James: And background. We have very similar backgrounds as well.

Emma: James, the truth about our industry, and you know this, is that it's impossible to start on the bottom rungs, because the pay is either non-existent or it's so minimal that you actually have to have someplace, probably in London, to live, which tends to be your parents'. And so, you know, most people have a certain socio-economic background and you can't even get into this industry because you can't make a living, which means that our voices have gone. Gone. There's a reason there aren't a huge amount of people from low socio-economic backgrounds who are running our channels, who are our gatekeepers.

Again, the toughest thing for me to admit here is that I have waxed lyrical for years about precisely what Emma is saying but I saw myself, incredibly, as a *victim* of what she describes. After leaving university, I had none of the trust funds or London boltholes that many of my friends enjoyed, and any of Dad's old mates who might have helped me onto a newspaper had either died or, like him, been made redundant. So I sold suits in a posh shop on London's Regent Street while knocking, with increasing desperation, on the doors of all the newspapers and broadcasters before finally sneaking through one.

You can tell by the way I still frame this explanation that I saw/see it as my prevailing over various disadvantages that my friends and future colleagues did not have to endure. That is why, for all its middle-class self-indulgence, I think my instinctive resentment of the idea that I enjoyed any 'white' privilege is born of the notion that this somehow negates my 'struggles' and my fear at the time that I might end up measuring rich men's inside legs for the rest of my life. If *I* can feel that resentment in my bones then it's hardly fair to castigate someone stuck in a rut they despise for furiously rejecting the idea that they enjoy what some tossers on the telly keep calling 'white privilege'. And yet, if something truly exists then no amount of denials or dismissals can ever make it untrue. It doesn't stop us trying, though.

James: It's worse now than it was when I left university.

Emma: It's much worse but I can tell you, after the coronavirus it's going to be even worse. So from my own perspective, we don't have a single show on TV that features a predominantly East Asian cast in any way. I've been trying to get that off the ground for years and years and years and the only way that you can do that is if you set a Chinese family in a restaurant, right? And that's because that is the British white idea of what Chinese people are, the setting that they should be in. And once you dehumanise people of a different colour, you set them apart, and you therefore say that they are not fully human. And therefore we can look at them and we can treat them differently. And we can look at them as exotic and say we don't understand them. And I think that distance makes it easier for people to step away when bad things happen to people of colour and say, 'Hey, I'm not racist! I have black friends, I have Chinese friends, I have whatnot.' But actually, when it comes to passing the mic and actually giving up those opportunities and insisting that a person of colour gets that job instead, they're not going to do it. Because let's face it, James, in our industry, it's so hard to get to the top. It's so hard to be successful. It's so hard to make money. Who, when they finally get their dream gig, is going to turn around and say, 'Actually, I shouldn't be writing this. I shouldn't be a white person writing a black narrative or a radio show about the Palestinian affair.' I'm a middle-aged white guy and I want to do this, right? So I'm not going to give up my platform and my money to somebody of colour. I'm going to do it myself and keep it to myself, even though all the opportunities of writing white narratives are also open to me and not open to them.

As I write this, the American actress Halle Berry has just garnered a collection of compliments and criticisms for withdrawing from a film in which she had been cast as a trans man. People I like and admire contended that it was a ridiculous decision because she is an *actress* and therefore every role she plays involves her pretending to be something and someone she is not. I was leaning towards agreeing with them until I listened back to what Emma just said about avenues remaining open. It puts a completely different complexion on what had seemed to me to be a fairly straightforward issue. There will be nothing to stop Berry playing a trans man when trans men are routinely cast in roles that nobody would currently consider them for. She, meanwhile, remains spoiled for choice. To mess with your head still further, Berry is, of course, a woman of colour.

James: I think I need to defend a few of the points that you make, although I wouldn't even dream of seeking to defend all of them. It's not a decision that you get to make. If I resigned on air *now*, I'd have absolutely no influence whatsoever over who replaced me. So you, you perhaps oversimplify the personal battles that many of us face. So that would be point number one. Point number two would be, we don't have conversations about the Palestinian experience or the East Asian experience every day; we take a majority view on conversation, some of which I'm supremely qualified to talk about. For example, I don't know, institutional child sexual abuse in Catholic schools. Some subjects I have to rely upon my callers to educate me, which is why you're back on the programme today. To suggest that you have to have an exclusively ethnicity-based worldview in order to conduct a certain type of conversation might be fair, but there's no earthly way that anybody is exclusively qualified to host 15 hours of conversation and interaction every week. So I've got a problem with that. And the key point of all is that if I ran a radio station, I would be in charge of who was on it. But I'm not.

Emma: James, this is why I started my last call by saying that I listen every day. I love the way that you look at the world and talk about things. You are incredibly open and you're open-minded in a way that means you will take on board what your callers say.

James: I got this wrong. I got this horribly, horribly wrong. I treated you, I think, inappropriately. I don't know if it was rude, I would have to listen back, but I completely misunderstood and rode roughshod over your point. I'm absolutely guilty of that. But I'm still a white bloke who went to public school and has his dream job in the media. And that's part of the problem for you.

Emma: It is part of the problem. And this is where the fear of being incredibly uncomfortable comes in. Because when you have privilege, equality feels like oppression. There's a reason why people at Eton are the ruling class. They actually believe that that is what they're destined to be.

James: The other problem for me is that what you also do – and I'm very, very conscious of this, possibly more conscious than you are – you also create a narrative in which people who we would both be opposed to now get to shout at people like me: 'Oh! Well, if you care that much you'd resign your job.' It's a bit like saying, 'If you *really* care about refugees, you would have one in your spare bedroom.' 'If you love the European Union so much, why don't you move there?' And so it follows:

'If you really care about racism, why don't you resign and replace yourself with a person of colour?' Now, leaving aside the absolute impossibility of me being able to do that, you've just given some serious ammunition to people that we would both be opposed to, haven't you?

Emma: I would never want you to give up your job.

James: But don't just talk about me. Talk about the idea that the only meaningful way ...

Emma: But we are talking about you specifically because you are getting targeted online right now.

James: Again, for the avoidance of confusion, this is not what I describe as being targeted. You're here because I thought about what you said and thought that I'd got it wrong. If you want to see 'targeted' have a look at what Nazi Twitter has to say about me! Don't worry about me. Ever. But that is the problem, isn't it? Somehow, in order to retain my integrity, in order for a white anti-racist to retain their integrity, they should give their job to a person of colour. You're pretty close to saying that.

Emma: What I'm saying is that this is the systemic situation that we're in right now. This is the infrastructure that precludes the people that can speak out most and at least change the narrative and change the way that our audiences view black people and people of different ethnicities. That is the problem. Now, I guess for you, and for other people who have a privileged position who are white, the only thing I could say is that every time you're thinking about getting a guest, or you're thinking about somebody who's going to come on your show and have a platform, please think about who that person is. And if it is a middle-aged white guy, perhaps just make a little bit more of an effort to reach out and find voices that wouldn't normally be the person that you would think about reaching out for on that subject. Think about the stereotype of people of colour, and the ethnicities, and then say actually, you know, rather than have this white, middle-aged, male barrister from a certain background, why don't we start to look out for women of colour from another socio-economic background who are also doing this job, and get them on this platform and raise their profile. And let's hear about this issue from their point of view, from their worldview, from their background and their work and their angle. So that we actually hear somebody else's voice and they might have a completely different take on what a rich, white, male, public-school-educated barrister or lawyer or politician or any of these people might have to say about the issue that you want to discuss. That, I think, is the biggest takeaway that I could ask of anybody who's in a position of privilege, who is white, if they want to make a difference. Start reaching out, hiring, giving money and giving platforms to people of colour that we'd never normally hear on our radio stations and on our screens and start saying, 'We want to hear your voice. I want to hear what you're saying, what your story is, without being editorialised or talked down to or censored.'

James: And if people call it 'positive discrimination', then just tell them to jog on?

Emma: The level playing field doesn't exist. Already with coronavirus, if you don't have a garden you already are not on an equal playing field in terms of your mental health, how you live with everything, right? The level playing field doesn't exist. So I'm all for quotas and for helping people who do not have the same opportunities.

I thought previously that I was in favour of the second half of Emma's final sentence while strenuously opposed to the first half. I see now that you can't be one without being the other. How else will society move toward a more equal footing for every member until our culture and our media reflect the wider realities of our population's identities? I still don't think 'white privilege' is the perfect term to describe the process by which I can bridle at the suggestion that a TV channel would prefer a black version of me while someone on the other side of the tracks is outraged by the suggestion that he has any privilege at all. We're both in denial, though, and until we're not, 'white privilege' will remain the best way of describing what it is we're denying.

Chapter 5

TATTOOS, PRIVATE SCHOOLS AND MARRIAGE

IT SEEMS UNLIKELY THAT the three subjects under scrutiny here have ever been lumped together quite like this before but, for me at least, they have something important in common. I am quite wrong about all of them. I know this and yet, even as I write these words, I am aware that somewhere deep inside me, somewhere still immune to all the facts, evidence and empathy in the world, I still somehow think that I am 'right'. I would not want my children to be taught or my country policed by someone with visible tattoos; I do not think fee-paying or grammar schools should be abolished; and I believe that couples who have not formally pledged their commitment to each other in some sort of ceremony are in inferior relationships to those of us who have. I know. I sound like a bigot.

My usual toolbox of tactics is of little use. When I find myself or encounter others holding potentially unpleasant or unhealthy positions, I try to ask three questions: 'What are you afraid of?' 'What are you *really* angry about?' 'How would you feel if the roles were reversed?' It's obviously simplistic and far from foolproof and I know that many people who feel the foundations of their certainties crumble beneath their feet while live on my radio show don't actually change their views in that moment. Nevertheless, when you add empathy and lived experience to the mix you often achieve a level of clarity that might otherwise be elusive. It has served me well but it does nothing on these three apparently disparate issues. I would like to work out why because, while not as obviously 'important' as many of the other issues discussed here, I still think that self-scrutiny can be effective at depth despite being forged in the shallows.

To begin with: tattoos. It's hard to believe today, when the world and their wife has an ink or two, but when I was growing up they were still regarded as quite extraordinary in my bog-standard, middle-class milieu. Looking back, I see myself associating them with Hells Angels, football hooligans and other perceived troublemakers. However, like a lot of easily bored kids from my sort of background, I was generally drawn to bad behaviour and had an immature respect for subversion and what I would then have called 'rebellion'. I would, for example, flout uniform rules at school and rail against regimentation. From my teens, I remember worrying quite seriously about becoming a 'wage slave' or sacrificing my supposed individuality on the altar of conformity. I was no Ray Davies, though. I was a walking cliché. But for some reason, tattoos always turned me into Lady Bracknell.

Of course, these days my friends and colleagues have plenty, and very nice they are too. No doubt my own daughters will contemplate joining them soon enough. Yet whenever the newspapers find a primary school teacher or a police officer who has been disciplined for displaying theirs at work I *still* feel my hackles rise and come down squarely on the side of the employer.

Now, perhaps unlike a lot of people who phone me at work for a fight, I would really rather not feel this way – it's snobbish, silly and offensive. I can hardly object to scruffiness or portray myself as a paragon of smartness – especially since they introduced cameras to the radio studio a few years ago – but I can ignore all that and construct a fairly compelling case for tattoos compromising a tattooed person's ability to do their job. I want to stress first that it is wholly sincere. I do this stuff for a living and still can't tell whether a professional provocateur is speaking from the heart or with their eye fixed solely on the clicks/switchboard/comments section, but I promise there is nothing contrived about my dislike of body art. I also know that my prejudices would not stand up to the sort of scrutiny I normally enjoy inflicting on other people's. Like a lot of my callers, I've never properly examined the foundations on which my certainty is built. To be honest, I've never really thought about it at all. So I wonder how I would feel if the roles were reversed, if I were made to confront my own dodgy opinions.

I wonder what would happen if I could somehow phone in to my own show ...

Caller James: It's just not professional, James. I don't want my children being taught by someone who looks like they've scrawled all over themselves with felt-tip pens.

Host James: I see. So it's the aesthetics you object to? If we could find a teacher who had been tattooed by Leonardo da Vinci you'd be OK?

Caller: No. I just don't think it's appropriate for teachers to look so scruffy and ill-kempt when the children they teach are required to look smart. It sets a bad example.

Host: Even if they're brilliant teachers?

Caller: That's the point. If they didn't have the tattoo they'd be *even better* teachers than they are already.

Host: How come?

Caller: Well, they wouldn't have to overcome the children's fear or discomfort.

Host: Fear or discomfort of what?

Caller: Of the tattoos.

Host: Ah. So your objection to primary school teachers refusing to cover up their tattoos at work is based upon the idea that they frighten and discomfort the children?

Caller: Yes.

Host: Do you know any children who are frightened of tattoos?

I'm always encouraged, when someone else is on the receiving end of my sub-Socratic interrogations, by how rarely they lie. It would be quite easy to close the conversation down here by doing so and insisting that I know *hundreds* of children who break out in hives at the sight of any body art. With a few glorious exceptions my callers rarely do, though, so I will follow their example here. All that follows is true.

Caller: No.

Host: Are you? [Or, more precisely, 'What are you *really* afraid of?']

Caller: Am I what?

Host: Are you frightened of people with tattoos?

Caller: No. Of course not. I just don't think they set a good example to children.

Host: Tell me who you're thinking of when you talk about tattoos like that. There must be a person or persons in your mind's eye. Describe them to us.

Caller: (pauses) OK. There was a man in Kidderminster when I was growing up who had his entire face tattooed with a spider's web. We called him Spiderman and he was pretty scary.

Host: Did you ever interact with him?

Caller: Not really. My mum worked on the make-up counter in the local department store and one time, it must have been the school holidays, I went in to see her and this guy was spraying all the perfumes on himself. Looking back, he was probably on something. Anyway, my mum and her colleagues were really worried and they called over the security guard.

Host: And?

Caller: And he got a bit lairy and shouty but they led him out of the store and that was that.

Host: Did you see him again?

Caller: Oh, yes. He was quite a familiar figure around town when I was a kid.

Host: Would you say you were scared of him?

Caller: (pause) Yes. Yes, I was.

Host: And, off the top of your head, can you think of any other negative encounters you've ever had with tattooed people?

Caller: No.

Host: Do you like any people with tattoos?

Caller: Yes. Loads.

Host: Would you trust them to look after your children?

Caller: Yes, obviously. Their uncle has a tattoo. And two of their godmothers.

Host: So why would you have a problem with their teacher having one?

Caller: I don't know.

And I still don't. Until just now, I hadn't thought about Spiderman in 35 years but it seems likely that my prejudice stems at least in part from that early negative experience. My mum is a supremely unflappable human so seeing her so discombobulated clearly struck me hard at the time and stayed with me long afterwards. It hadn't crossed my mind that 'What are you afraid of?' might be the key to unlocking my own cognitive dissonance here, as it sometimes is with callers who phone in about less trivial topics. Incidentally, Mum's always maintained that my lifelong dislike of large slobbery dogs stems from the time she found me strapped in to my baby chair with a friend's Bassett Hound licking my face. It seems equally likely that associating tattoos with chaos and fear stems from that afternoon at the Estée Lauder concession in Kidderminster.

So now I know it I can fix it, right? Not necessarily. Here's a real call that took place a few years ago, during another discussion about a primary school teacher who had been ordered to cover up her body art.

James: Lauren, what would you like to say?

Lauren: I work with kids. I am a fantastic nurse with kids. I work in some of the best London hospitals for kids. My patients' families call me an angel. They say I'm a darling and then they notice that I've got tattoos and piercings in my neck.

There's a way of saying 'yes' that sounds so sneery it makes my blood boil when I hear other presenters doing it, especially when they use it in response to a caller's description of racism or homophobia they've personally experienced. It comes out like an elongated 'nyerss'. You must have heard it yourself. I'm surprised and ashamed to admit that when I dug out this recording from 2014 I heard myself making precisely the same noise at this point in the conversation.

> **James:** Nyerss. In your neck?
>
> **Lauren:** In my neck.
>
> **James:** How do they work? Is it like a fold of skin? You sort of pinch a fold of skin and then put a stud through it?
>
> **Lauren:** Yes.
>
> **James:** (sneering again) OK.
>
> **Lauren:** It doesn't affect my nursing.
>
> **James:** How could it affect your nursing?
>
> **Lauren:** Well, it doesn't affect the quality of my nursing but apparently a tattoo on a teacher would affect the quality of their teaching.
>
> **James:** No. It ... it ... Let me have a think. Um. If the kids aren't allowed to have tattoos, why should the teacher be?

This is clearly ridiculous but I am sincerely searching for some way, any way, to avoid admitting the wrongness of my original position. A bit of bluster, some attempted charm, a sort of knowing wink to my own desperation, all while trying to keep the argument alive.

Lauren: Because the teacher's an adult.

[I make a weird and prolonged kissing noise here. Seriously. Presumably because I couldn't think of anything to say and it seemed preferable to silence.]

Lauren: And they have their own money.

James: Yeah. Alright. Erm.

Lauren: And they have full rights over their own bodies. They don't have to call up their mums and say, 'Can I have a tattoo?'

James: OK. No one likes a bully, Lauren.

[In my defence, this is said more to amuse than to challenge but I'm stunned by the contortions I'm undertaking to avoid admitting that she's right. Lauren, quite rightly, laughs at me rather than with me.]

James: Erm …

(Pause.)

I must have a leg to stand on, mustn't I? On this? There must be something I can say. Let me see what the head teachers at the school said … Professional image! You can't have a professional image with a bolt in your neck.

Lauren: But I can and I do. They call me an angel. Doctors ask to work with me.

James: Has anyone ever had a word? Has anyone ever said, 'Are you sure about that neck-piercing, nurse?'

Lauren: No. No.

James: So what you've done to me is cast me in the role of a man who would say, 'I don't want that brilliant nurse coming anywhere near my daughter because she's got tattoos and a stud in her neck.'

Lauren: Yes. Why would you say that to me?

James: It's not a very nice role to be cast in, is it?

(Lauren chuckles.)

Remember that this was six years ago and I had forgotten all but the most basic details of my conversation with Lauren when I went to find it for this chapter. So, given the central thrust of this whole book, and the personal experiences that prompted it, I am a bit stunned by what I said next.

James: Alright. Um. You're a nurse. Obviously, you're not a fully qualified therapist but you're closer to it than I am. What's wrong with me? What's wrong with me?

(Pause.)

Lauren: Well. Maybe because you wouldn't choose to do it you can't see why others might choose to do it.

James: It's not that. There are lots of things I wouldn't choose to do but I've got absolutely no problem at all with other people doing them. There is something wrong with me. This is a bigoted position. This is a prejudice. This is discriminatory practice that I am currently favouring. What is wrong with me, Lauren? Actually, I'll say that again. What is wrong with me, nurse?

Lauren: (laughing, I think/hope, with me this time) I don't know. I'm not arguing with you. It is slightly bigoted, isn't it?

James: Slightly? This is the definition of bigoted. Here's loads and loads of evidence that I'm wrong but I'm still insisting that I'm right.

Lauren: It's your choice. Your choice.

James: It's my choice to be bigoted? It's my choice to be prejudiced? I never wanted to be that person.

And who, in all honesty, would want to be that person? A person, I think, who derives some comfort from the strength of his own certainties. Who keeps the chaos and unpredictability of life at bay by constructing apparently unshakeable positions which at least provide a semblance of simplicity and order. I took against tattoos at a very early age for a reason I've only just recognised and I spent the subsequent decades deriving some sort of comfort from the strength of my convictions. If I had kept them to myself perhaps they wouldn't have mattered but they led me to sit in ludicrous judgment on people like Lauren and the teacher in the story she rang in to discuss.

Don't laugh at this logical leap but, for me, the major historical problem with institutionalised religion is the licence it gives us to sit in judgment on other people's choices. Worse, the licence it gives leaders to determine the behaviour of followers, to impose strict conditions of what is 'right' and what is 'wrong' without ever being required to explain themselves or their reasoning. Worse still, they can foment a contagion of sententiousness that sees the 'faithful' delight in condemning the conduct of the non-believer. It bestows immense and unwarranted power on a select few and the problem clearly extends deep in to the secular world. There is some insecurity here too, an attempt to bury the fear, and I wonder whether the more insecurity one suffers the more one is likely to retreat into the comfort of false certainties. The trick with this is, I suppose, not to analyse your position too closely and to resist any attempts by others to do so. Ultimately, then, among the worst things you could do if you wanted to leave your views unchallenged would be to ring a radio show like mine. I sometimes worry that one of the best ways to keep the barricades against admitting wrongness high is to present one.

One of the most abiding lessons of my own therapy was that 'the teacher will appear when the student is ready'. As with much of what I've been through over the last few years, it's precisely the sort of sentiment that I would once have delighted in ridiculing. Today, I think I can unpack its quiet beauty here with reference to some things that happened to me, quite literally, yesterday. First, my publisher sent me a quote that he thought would help me clarify why I feel so strongly about using the platforms I currently have to try to help people suffering from problems similar to my own. And, more pertinently, why I think baring some of my own secret soul is the most effective way I can achieve this ambition. It is advice given by the late American comedy genius Garry Shandling to his then protégé, the writer and film director Judd Apatow, and it states simply that: 'The more personal it is, the more universal it is.'

Second, my eldest daughter bounded into my room later in the day to excitedly announce that a film co-written by and starring one of our favourite young artists, Pete Davidson of *Saturday Night Live* fame, had just been released for streaming. *The King of Staten Island* lived up to our dizziest expectations and provided much-needed relief from the coronavirus lockdown and some struggles I was having with this chapter. It beautifully deploys elements of Davidson's own life – his fireman father was killed in the Twin Towers and he is bipolar and suffers from attention deficit disorder – to explore broader issues of love, trust and redemption. Avoiding any spoilers, Davidson's character dreams of being a tattoo artist and, in a bizarre act of love, his mother's estranged straight-laced boyfriend offers him his own back to practise on. So, in a tale that seeks to make the deeply personal universal, not only are tattoos rendered the opposite of scary and subversive, they actively become loving and special.

I was processing the happy coincidence of watching a film focused on tattooing at the end of a day I had spent writing about tattoos as the credits rolled. *The King of Staten Island* was co-written and directed by Judd Apatow. I think that's what the line about the teacher and the student means. If you can get your mind more open – even just ajar! – and receptive to change then you will notice alignments and lessons that would otherwise go unheeded. It remains to be seen whether Spiderman, Lauren, Pete Davidson and Judd Apatow will combine to create a completely different reaction in me when the next story about a tattooed teacher appears in the newspapers but I'm optimistic now. I'll have to let you know.

Unfortunately, I can't currently see any comparable celluloid help on the horizon for the issue which brings out my inner Victorian more than any other: marriage. It is an issue on which I find myself agreeing with people whom I consider to be profoundly wrong about almost everything else and it has brought me into direct conflict with some of the people I love most in the world. For reasons I have, again, never really tried to unpick, I remain convinced that a formal union between two people of any sex or sexuality (it doesn't have to be religious, just legal) constitutes a 'gold standard' of relationships that can simply not be applied to any others. It is a plainly ridiculous and deeply offensive position. It insults loving families the world over and completely ignores the simple fact that a 'piece of paper' says nothing at all about the depth or sincerity of a commitment. Yet I genuinely and quite passionately 'believe' it. So here I am. Stuck in the riddle – presumably without you.

To try my three favourite keys again, I don't *think* I'm actively angry about anything here or scared of some deeply buried memory, so we'll try the idea of roles being reversed, of me being on the receiving end of my own pig-headedness.

Host: So you genuinely think that, just by dint of being married, your relationship is objectively superior to mine? That your children are somehow growing in a healthier, more loving environment than mine?

Caller: Not necessarily more loving, but healthier? Yes.

Host: Why?

Caller: Because they know that me and their mum are in it for the long haul, that we're committed to each other and won't be splitting up. That obviously makes for a more secure childhood.

Host: You've heard of divorce?

Caller: Yes, but the statistics show that parents who are married are less likely to split up than parents who are not.

Host: Correlation is not the same as causation and there are lots of other factors in play on this specific issue but OK.

Park that. Do you think that the children of divorced parents are less secure or growing up in a less healthy environment than the children of unmarried parents who are still together?

Caller: No.

Host: So marriage *per se* has not delivered any protection or advantage to those children?

Caller: Again, they had a better chance of their parents staying together because their parents were married.

Host: And again, that's too simplistic. Parents who are struggling financially are less likely to get married and parents who are struggling financially are more likely to split up. You're moulding the statistics to fit your opinion. I'm interested in where the opinion comes from. Did you feel this way about marriage before you read anything about these numbers?

Caller: Yes. I've felt this way since I was a kid.

Host: So your parents were married?

Caller: Yes.

Host: Any friends or family members with parents who weren't?

Caller: No. I don't think so. This was the 1970s. A few people we knew got divorced but I think they were all married to start with.

Host: And the children of the parents who got divorced, were they hurt or damaged by the experience?

Caller: Yes. Some of them, I think.

Host: Would they have been more or less hurt if their parents hadn't been married in the first place?

Caller: I don't know. I don't think it would have made any difference.

Host: So marriage itself doesn't actually have any bearing on how children feel when their parents split up?

Caller: No. Probably not.

Host: And if the parents stay together for the duration, will the children be more or less secure and happy according to whether their parents are married?

Caller: Retrospectively? When we know that the parents *have* stayed together?

Host: Yes.

Caller: I don't think it would make any difference at all.

Host: Apart from ones imposed by social convention or your own prejudice, you don't think the children of the unmarried, still together parents suffer any disadvantage compared to the married, still together parents?

Caller: What prejudice?

Host: The one you rang in with. The idea that the kids whose parents are together but not married are fruits of a relationship that is not 'gold standard'.

Caller: Oh. No. I mean yes. I don't think the children of un-married but together parents are at any disadvantage.

Host: So it's not about gold standards, then. You said your parents were married?

Caller: Yes.

Host: Would they have loved you any less if they hadn't been?

Caller: No.

Host: Would they have been less good parents if they hadn't been married?

Caller: No.

Host: Again, leaving aside social mores and snobbery, would you have been objectively less happy and secure if everything about your childhood had been identical to what it was except for the fact that your parents never got married?

Caller: Well, you might have got teased or bullied about it in that era but other than that, no. I don't think so. No.

Host: So why does it matter so much to you?

I think I know the answer to this. I can feel it forming in my mind and I am, to be honest, a little bit scared of it. While having this internal dialogue I am hearing echoes of how Mum and Dad explained why my biological mother gave me up for adoption. At its simplest, the explanation was that she believed my mum and dad could give me a better life than she ever could. Thus, giving me up was, in my mind and in my memory, *always* an act of love. They never spoke about me being 'unwanted', only about me being 'chosen', and I think now that my child-hood calculations must have led me to attach enormous impor-tance to the things that distinguished my mum and dad from my biological mother (I'm not sure the father ever knew she was pregnant). By far the most obvious being that she was not married. So being married *must* be better than everything else, I must have decided, and this was one of the main reasons why I was given to Mum and Dad. I have to believe that marriage is a 'gold standard' because if I'd been born into a society that treated a teenage single mum with the same respect and decency that it treats a married couple contemplating parenthood then perhaps I would not have been adopted by my parents, in which case I would, literally, not be me.

Host: So why does it matter so much to you?

Caller: Because if we didn't treat married couples as somehow intrinsically superior to unmarried couples or even single mums then I wouldn't have been given to Mum and Dad and that is the single most awful thing I can imagine happening to baby me.

Host: Wow. That doesn't really qualify you to comment on anyone else's circumstances though, does it? It doesn't give you the right to sit in judgement on other people's relationships or talk about 'gold standards' or categorise my relationship as inferior to yours, does it?

Caller: No. No, it really doesn't. I'm sorry.

I'm not suggesting that you should start conducting imaginary radio phone-ins with yourself but there is, I hope, a lesson here for all of us. Asking ourselves questions about why we feel or think certain things is the surest way of moving the needle on the dial of our opinions. Of course, it presumes a desire on at least some level to examine our thinking and that is certainly not the case with many of the people who ring my show. But the principle holds.

Whether you are addressing your wounded inner child or conversing with a 'spirit guide' or phoning a real radio show for a scrap, these sorts of self-examination can be incredibly liberating. The older I get, the more convinced I become that you can't argue anyone into changing their mind, you can simply question them into a place where they will be able to do it for themselves. If we hold an opinion that regularly brings us into conflict with people we care for or even with our own consciences then it is probably doing us harm. Whether we realise it or not. I remember looking at my gorgeous nephew on his parents' wedding day and *knowing* that I was a dick for thinking it mattered at all that they hadn't been married when he was born. And yet at the same time, even there, I couldn't shake the conviction. I think I can now. So, to all the people I've badgered on the radio and all the people listening who've felt judged and insulted, I'm really sorry. Of course it's love and commitment and kindness that matter most. Ultimately, marriage really is just a piece of paper and an excuse for a massive party. (I would, however, still urge you to swot up on the wildly different legal statuses of married and unmarried people when it comes to splitting up. Sorry to be unromantic.)

And so to school. From the age of three to eighteen, my parents paid for me to go to exclusively (and indeed exclusive) fee-paying ones. For many years, I felt the burning injustice of them being able to buy me advantages over others and would argue furiously for their abolition. And yet of all the views that Dad, to my intense annoyance, used to insist I would grow out of this was the one he was most certain of. And he was, as usual, right. Up to a point.

Selective education is unfair. Whether financial or exam-based, it is an appalling obstacle to social mobility and equality. It is plainly ridiculous that one child should have a better education than another because that child's parents have more money or because they passed an exam before they were teenagers.

And yet, when it comes to education, I know I am a hypocrite and, in all honesty, I don't want to change. Even though I understand that the sort of social mobility I dream of for our society simply cannot be achieved while access to the finest schools in the land is in any way based upon money or exams passed at the age of eleven. But when I give my children the best possible schooling we can afford or access, I don't see how I could honestly campaign to deny other people opportunities I took for myself and my daughters. I know that the sort of schools I went to, for all their flaws and failings in the present and especially the past, bestow a sense of entitlement and possibility that is of great value in our society. My mum and dad sent me to those schools because they saw that entitlement and belief in the possibility of things propel other people into places they themselves had to work much harder to reach. And as long as the advantages bestowed remain so considerable, I am simply not principled or morally strong enough to contemplate sacrificing my children's future on the altar of my politics.

In a world where we increasingly seem to think that a person is either wholly good or wholly bad, it feels important to me that we own our flaws, our failings. I hope this isn't a cop out.

I used to think that grammar schools – state-funded but rigorously selective on supposedly academic grounds – provided a path out of the hypocrisy but I was wrong about that too. In their current incarnations, they're just as divisive and unfair as fee-paying schools. If you can afford pre-entrance exam private tuition or to move into the relevant catchment area, where houses prices are always inflated, you're simply securing a different flavour of unfair advantage. I used to defend grammar schools not, I see now, because of any objective good that they provide but because I figured that if the cards had fallen differently in my own life I would have got into one and still benefited from an education measurably superior to that available to less 'intelligent' children.

I often think that the peculiar obsessions many on the uglier side of right-wing politics have with me come from the fact that I am unquestionably qualified to describe the inequality perpetuated by a system designed to bestow *even more* advantage on the most privileged members of our society because I benefited from it. This means that they can't accuse me of envy and, in this context, the lazy 'champagne socialist' label doesn't work at all. They know that when I criticise prominent right-wing politicians I am speaking from a position of lived experience. I *know* that these men (for they are almost always men) would not be in the positions they inhabit today if their parents had not, like mine, paid for them to have a head start in life. I don't know why these types find it so hard to admit the role that dumb luck has played in their ascents – born on third base, as Americans like to say. Interestingly, exactly the same sort of people often have an enormous problem with the very concept of 'white privilege'. It's not hard to see what both positions have in common. Just like my own parents, though, I will not leave the field of superior education and all the life advantages it entails clear for them and their ilk while I have the resources to provide it for me and mine.

I'm not sure whether I'm calling my next witness for the prosecution or the defence of my position but he is such an interesting contributor that I will leave that question hanging. Sir Nicholas Soames, a grandson of Winston Churchill and Conservative MP, took to phoning the show a few years ago on a variety of topics. Having quickly realised that there was rather more to 'Nick in Westminster' than the description allowed, I found him to be a charming and thoughtful contributor. A poster boy of sorts for 'inherited privilege', he nonetheless possesses a sense of public duty that causes me to question some of my lazier assumptions about class and entitlement. On this occasion, Education Secretary Damian Hinds had announced that he wanted to help state-educated children from normal backgrounds achieve what he described as a 'public school swagger'. It was shorthand, I think now, for the sort of entitlement and sense of possibility described above but Sir Nicholas was, to say the least, unimpressed. It is a fascinating exchange which, I hope, shows that availing one-self of opportunities not available to everybody is not necessarily the mark of a scoundrel. It's also possible, of course, that I'm citing my friendly ribbing of Soames to salve my own conscience.

Soames: I rather object to Damian Hinds, who is my friend and who I like.

James: Yes.

Soames: I object to this 'public school swagger'. I don't think that's true. I don't know what they mean by public school swagger. Unfortunately, I didn't go to university. I wanted to be a soldier. I went straight from Eton to the army and I can tell you that whatever swagger I may have had was kicked out of me in quick time in the first three weeks I was in the army.

James: Well, not quite as robustly as it would have been if you'd gone in as a squaddie instead of going to Sandhurst, Sir Nicholas.

Soames: No, everyone has the stuffing kicked out of them when they go into the army.

James: Different types of stuffing, surely?

Soames: No, they inculcate discipline and a series of values that you don't have as a young man.

James: Yes, but you were being inculcated with whatever you would need to become a member of the officer class so it's going to be a very different inculcation from what it would have been for the rank and file.

Soames: Everyone goes through the same basic training.

James: Alright, I'm not going to argue with you about what happens in the army. I'll argue with you about most things but not about what goes on in the army.

Soames: The point I'm trying to make is that I really do wish that – and I acknowledge that I had incredible life chances and I'm extremely grateful, very fortunate, don't think I don't know it – I really do wish that governments were able at the drop of a light switch to improve the opportunities that stem from other types of schooling. It's about excellence and it's about leadership at the top of schools. Now, I'm in my constituency today in Mid Sussex. I'm visiting a school that has just had the most fantastic Ofsted inspection which just highlights, you know, leadership, opportunity – all the things which these young men and women are getting at this school and I don't see why this shouldn't be the same at every school in the land. I really don't. And I don't like it that it isn't.

James: I'm going to ambush you slightly here and I'm going to speculate that you wouldn't send your own children there.

(Long pause. Long enough to make me wonder, for a moment, whether the line had gone down.)

Soames: Well, you've bowled me middle stump. I sent my children to public schools. That is true. But I'm trying not to personalise the conversation ...

James: Of course. I'm going to take your phrase and move forward with it. Life chances. Now, with the greatest of respect, in the annals of privilege by birth you knock me into a cocked hat but we both acknowledge that life chances are something that were bought for us by dint of the schools that we went to.

Soames: I acknowledge that and my particular thing is that I really, passionately believe that this kind of excellence in education is achievable through leadership, through quality of teaching and through aspiration. And I see in these schools in my constituency parents who really get involved and are driving excellence forward with brilliant teachers.

James: So it's doable?

Soames: It is doable. And it's inexcusable that we don't do it better and don't do it more.

James: So the phrase 'public school swagger', although built on the best of intentions, is a profoundly unhelpful way of describing what we're discussing.

Soames: I think it's a really unhelpful thing to say and I shall tell Damian when I next see him. I just don't think it means anything. I know a lot of fellows who've got absolutely no bloody swagger at all. They need to stand up and take their hands out of their pockets. What matters is the quality and the aspiration. Really, I think, the determination of these schools to tell these young people that the world is their oyster. And that, I think, is what you get at a public school.

He is absolutely right, of course. That is exactly what you get at the sort of schools we both attended. The problem, for me, lies in the question of whether all the other schools will really be able to scale similar heights of aspiration while ones like ours exist. Like Soames, my brain says yes. Unlike him, my conscience still says no and that is why being 'wrong' can be so hard to admit and so hard to live with. We are all hypocrites, and if you're not willing or able to actually change then the next best thing we can do is surely to admit it.

Chapter 6
FATTY FATTY FAT FATS

NOT LONG AFTER BECOMING a full-time broadcaster, I started to devote a lot of airtime to bullying and abusing over-weight people. I coined the phrase 'Fatty Fatty Fat Fats' to describe them and would, in what I considered at the time to be hilarious and edgy comedic monologues, routinely deride and mock not only people living with obesity, but also state-sponsored attempts to help them address their problems.

Listening back to one of the few surviving recordings for the first time in over a decade, I can't quite believe my ears. The tried and trusted tactic of imagining how I would feel if the roles were reversed – if I was morbidly obese and some self-appointed arbiter of taste and decorum on the radio was not only abusing me and my condition, but also enthusiastically encouraging his listeners to laugh at me – makes me feel pathetic and deeply ashamed. I remember one email corre-spondent at the time who would write to me weekly about how hurtful she found my material, how complex her own relationship with food had always been and how confident she was that I would respond to her calm and reasoned explanation of why what I was doing was so very wrong. She had, I'm afraid, rather too much faith in my decency.

After a while, I stopped responding to her lengthy and detailed pleas because, I think now, I was guilty of a sin that I have castigated other people for committing without ever realising that I had been just as guilty of it myself. I didn't mean *her*, you see. I didn't mean actual people with actual feelings and complicated, often unexplored reasons for engaging in what is in effect a form of self-harm. When I spoke of 'Fatty Fatty Fats Fats', always with a snide little giggle in my voice, I was talking of cartoonish caricatures. I could sustain the bizarre blend of vitriol and cruel humour because I had somehow dehumanised the people I was referring to, robbing them of individuality and lumping them all into an amorphous mass undeserving of sympathy, understanding or kindness.

I was not exactly thin myself at the time and would use this as a form of cover for my cruelty. Insisting that everyone with a weight problem needed simply to 'eat less and exercise more' may have been true in my own case but it was crass and ignorant to present it as a catch-all solution to problems that are often Gordian knots of mental health, self-esteem and myriad other issues. But I didn't see this at the time. I saw a mix of harmless fun and necessary criticism and would furiously reject the idea that I was being bigoted or stupid or cruel. Besides, some of my best friends were fat . . .

One of the most poignant refrains on the radio show in the immediate aftermath of the Brexit vote came from people, born in other EU countries, who had been told by friends, colleagues and even family members that they had voted to leave because there were 'too many immigrants' from the EU in the UK. They would point out to their workmates, their drinking buddies, their mother-in-law that they themselves were EU immigrants and, without fail, they received in return the bizarre explanation, 'Oh! I don't mean *you*.' It was, unsurprisingly, not a very comforting explanation and yet it was one which these people genuinely thought valid. The 'problem' immigrants, for them, were generally not the ones they had actually met and liked but those on the front pages and Nigel Farage's despicable 'Breaking Point' poster: the faceless, nameless hordes demonised by racist demagogues and newspaper editors. These people could not even begin to see how successfully they had been manipulated into a position of base xenophobia because, after all, their colleagues, their family members, even some of their best friends were immigrants ...

And so it was, for me, with overweight people. I could argue that the stakes were not as high, the consequences not as far-reaching, but I honestly believe now that the approach I took to obesity at the beginning of my broadcasting career bears all the hallmarks of the lazy, hate-filled, self-serving rhetoric that I have been railing against ever since.

In other words, when I used to talk about fat people I used to deploy *precisely* the same tactics and rationales that other people use to deride and demonise other minorities. It's a pretty grim admission but also, I hope, a helpful one. If a chap who routinely gallops in on his high horse to police other people's bigotries and prejudices can acknowledge his own and work out where they came from, it may provide a sort of template for deconstructing deliberately divisive rhetoric.

I really meant it, by the way, at least in my own mind. The abuse of obese people was no insincere playing to an appreciative gallery, which is how I suspect some professional provocateurs operate. Cruelty for clicks, if you like. On the contrary, I would argue my case on TV discussion shows and, even when actually confronted with someone who would, say, comfort eat to drown out memories of childhood abuse, I could easily retain the smug superiority that galls me so profoundly when I see it on other people's faces. Like them, I would close my eyes and put my fingers in my ears.

In January 2009, I opened one of my shows with a monologue. It doesn't make me feel great to do so, but I am going to reproduce it here as I think it might be helpful for me to expose it to the sort of 'forensic scrutiny' I try to bring to other people's similarly poisonous positions. I knew I was going to write about this, but until I started to marshal my thoughts here I hadn't fully realised that this monologue is so of a piece with other examples of hate speech and othering. Listening back, I struggle to believe that it's me, but the slickness of delivery, the linguistic levity and the tone throughout make it abundantly clear that I was *really* enjoying myself. It seems important to stress this. Like the school bully who thrives on the laughter of onlookers, I remember how uplifted and proud I felt when people told me how funny they found my 'fatty fatty fat fat' jibes. One caller, a mother, delightedly told me that her young daughter had pointed at another customer in the supermarket checkout queue and announced: 'Look, Mummy, a fatty fatty fat fat!' I found this utterly hilarious and loved the idea that an epithet coined by me was moving into wider circulation.

The top of the show is, traditionally, a call to arms. The idea is to grab the audience's attention and keep it. I hope these days that I do so by appealing to a listener's sense of curiosity or even justice, by promising to provide them with the information and insights they need to reach a properly informed opinion about the issues of the day. It is, of course, easier and often more popular to appeal to altogether baser instincts.

Don't panic yet! OK? It's not national. It only currently affects 300 people in Kent. Eastern and Coastal Kent Primary Care Trust to be precise — in conjunction with an organisation, a private company, called Weight Wins which runs incentive schemes for firms to encourage staff to lose weight. If successful, it is claimed, the scheme could be expanded across the country.

Already, then, the alarm has been sounded. There is a threat just over the horizon. It may not be time to panic *yet* and the numbers are relatively small but 'they' (and 'they' can, of course, refer to any misrepresented form of authority, expertise or vaguely described and conspiracy-theory-founded enemy of your interests) are poised to do you harm.

> *'What scheme?' I hear you cry. Well, just wait and I'll tell you. It's a scheme to give people money, via the NHS, therefore taxpayers' money, if they lose weight. Leaving aside for a moment how clearly this discriminates against people who are slender because they have no option to join in on this. You've got to be a major fatty fatty fat fat to qualify. It's no good if you're just a couple of pounds overweight. How do I know this? Well, because the rubric, the small print, is fairly specific.*

You see here that I am already casting myself in the role of trusted friend while encouraging you to despise people you've never met. I have the information that you need to fully understand the threat to your interests and I want to share it with you. The actual facts matter nowhere near as much as the feelings of grievance and even anger that I am trying to engender, but I have a mission, nay a duty, to share these 'facts' with you because I care about your welfare while the people 'in charge' (the Establishment) categorically do not. That's why it's so important to get the old 'taxpayers' money' canard front and centre as quickly as possible. The 'fatty fatty fat fat' phrase has already kicked off the othering process – most overweight people listening are already edging towards the conviction that I don't mean *them* – and the taxpayer line seeds the idea that this othered minority has got designs on resources, in this case money, that is rightfully yours.

I might as well be talking about desperate human beings reduced to risking their lives in flimsy dinghies in the English Channel. It's precisely the same tactic that can be used in the othering of any minority said to have designs on other resources – housing, benefits, jobs, etc – that are rightfully *yours*. The fundamental unfairness of this redistribution of funds will only become clear when you understand the finer detail and that's where I come in, pretending to be your friend with the facts but really just harvesting your negative emotions for money and/or power.

If you lose 15 pounds – how much is that? Is that more than a stone? It's quite a lot, isn't it? How many bags of sugar is that? If you lose 15 pounds – how many pounds in a stone? Fourteen? Any advance on 14? So that's just over a stone. If you lose just over a stone you will receive 70 notes. Seventy quid for losing 15 pounds. If you manage to shed – and you'd have to be a pretty lardy geezer to have this amount of spare luggage – if you manage to shed 30 pounds, guess how much you get for shedding 30 pounds? You get another 90 pounds. So the running total if you've shed 30 pounds is 160 pounds. I'm going to say 'quid' for the money otherwise it gets confusing, alright?

I'm not indulging in the vernacular or endorsing the use of slang but you could get a bit confused if I talk about losing 30 pounds and gaining 160 pounds so I'm going to say 'quids' for 'pounds.' Quids for pounds henceforth. So if you manage to shed 30 pounds of weight you get 160 quid. OK? If you manage to shed 50 pounds – 50 pounds! Fifty pounds! That's practically four stone. If you manage to shed 50 pounds of weight under this scheme that's been rolled out in Kent you will receive 425 knicker! Four hundred and twenty five spondulix! Four hundred and twenty five big ones! Four hundred and twenty five quid! For losing 50 pounds.

Just look at my 'man of the people' credentials! No matter that I went to public school and can currently spend more money on a dinner out than some people earn in a week (and more than you would get for losing 15 pounds), I am categorically *on your side*. You can tell by my 'hail fellow well met' demeanour and my deft deployment of faux confusion and funny slang terms. And the more you laugh at my verbal gymnastics, the more confident you can be that I won't be turning my acid tongue on you next. The more closely you ally yourself with me and my bullying and othering, the safer you will be from similar treatment. We're all in this together. And anyway, it's just a bit of harmless fun. It's not *real people* that we're laughing at. It's not 15 pounds of human being that we're talking about here, after all, it's just bags of sugar. Refugees aren't *real* people fleeing war and famine, they're *illegal immigrants* with designs on your birthright.

What a load of nonsense! Listen, I'm not at my fighting weight at the moment. I don't know about you but I'm carrying a little bit of extra luggage. Actually, I'm way over the mark. I reckon if I lost 30 pounds I'd be in peak condition. Now, I'm saying this I think quite modestly, quite, um, honestly, expecting the colleagues who sit in my eyeline to start shaking their heads vigorously but Amanda, who's producing the programme today, has just nodded quite sagely with a very serious look on her face. So if my natural joie de vivre and bonhomie seep out of my delivery over the course of the next ten minutes, blame her! You're not supposed to nod. She says, 'I would have said 15 pounds.' Is that supposed to make me feel better? OK. Fifteen pounds. So I would qualify for 70 quid. It ain't going to work, is it? I don't know whether it's because you need to have a sum of money on the table that is slightly mind-boggling. You need to be offered hundreds or thousands of pounds. If you offered me ten grand to lose a stone I'd have it off by the end of the weekend but, I don't know, 70 quid to get 15 pounds off? Let's examine this.

More chummy banter. There's even a wheezy giggle or two on the tape. Indeed, throughout this grisly monologue I sound absolutely delighted with myself. If I was made of chocolate, as the saying goes, I would undoubtedly have eaten myself. Because I'm such a 'good bloke', you see, even bringing my off-air colleagues into proceedings and taking the mickey out of myself. Besides, you cannot really be bullying fat people if you're fat yourself! The contradiction of casting the money available as simultaneously *too much* (to spend on fat people) and *too little* (to be an effective inducement) goes unnoticed because you're not supposed to think about this sort of thing, you're just supposed to *feel* it.

I'm interested – and oddly for this programme, where experience is generally considered more valuable than opinion – I am just interested in what you think of this story. I'm interested in whether you think it will work. Bearing in mind at the moment, of course, that if you're dying and there are drugs available that could prolong your life then under the auspices of many primary care trusts at the moment, you actually can't get them. You suffer the horror and indignity of knowing that if you lived, for example, in Scotland you would be in receipt of drugs that would prolong your life, but where you live you cannot get them on the NHS. What you can get instead – if you're a fatty fatty fat fat – is 425 pounds of taxpayer' money. Should we be spending NHS cash on a scheme like this? Call 0845 6060973. And perhaps more importantly, do you think it will work? Do you actually think that a financial incentive could encourage you or a fatty fatty fat fat of your acquaintance to shed a few pounds? In other words, will receiving money help you lose weight? I just want to know! And, I suppose, in order to – I was going to say put some flesh on the bones but that's a slightly unfortunate turn of phrase – in order to examine this a little further I'd like to know what it was for you that prompted you to take the plunge, as it were.

This is objectively gross but, again, a perfect illustration of how hateful rhetoric worms its way into the hearts and mouths of otherwise decent people. I am, with a straight face, suggesting that terminally ill people will die sooner than necessary because 'fatty fatty fat fats' are receiving money that should have been spent on lifesaving drugs. Don't laugh, but this is exactly how Brexit happened years afterwards. That ridiculous bus with its blatant lie about £350 million being suddenly available for the NHS if we stopped 'sending' it to Brussels never stood up to the scantest intellectual scrutiny but my goodness it provoked such powerful *feelings*. Feelings of grievance, of injustice, of anger and unfairness. Facts had absolutely nothing to do with any of it. Just as money spent on treating obesity would, in the long run, *save* fortunes for the NHS and the 'taxpayer', so the cost of EU membership was as nothing compared to its financial benefits.

Brexit is, obviously, a pet subject of mine but this analysis applies equally well to any example of people being persuaded to vote against their own interests by protagonists who knit together blatant lies with carefully cultivated scapegoats and

bogus tales of unfairness and victimhood. Demonising for-
eigners, whether they are exercising mythical 'power' over us
or simply 'coming over here' to help themselves to our stuff,
initially seems markedly different from demonising fat people.
It isn't, of course. Swap the word 'demonise' for 'dehumanise'
and the song remains the same.

More, rather than seducing you into doing something
wrong, I cast myself as encouraging you to do something *right*.
We need to stand together against both the architects and the
beneficiaries of this blatant unfairness, I am saying. No matter
that you hadn't even been aware of it until I told you, it's clear
that *something must be done*. And if a little qualm of conscience
starts whispering in the back of your mind, don't worry, I've
got your back. It's not really about *us*, you see. The 'taxpayer'
gambit might be designed to promote the notion that *we* are
losing what the fat people are getting but we're not actually
selfish or greedy. Oh no, we really care about the terminally ill
people. (Or, depending on which lie is being told, we really
care about the fishing industry, or the 'white working class', or
'Judeo-Christian values'.) I'm not actually attacking anyone,
you see, I'm protecting you. And my goodness you really need
protecting. The threat is all around us and you haven't even
noticed ...

*Obesity's all over the news today, I've got to tell you. There's
another story about a fireman who has lost his job on the
grounds of failing to get fit. He was given a warning that*

he was too fat to be a fireman. He has now had his dismissal from his post confirmed after failing to get in shape. There's a story about two-year-olds receiving NHS treatment – two-year-olds – receiving NHS treatment for obesity. It's a fatty fatty fat fat fiesta! But we'll begin with the question of whether or not we think a cash incentive could get you into losing weight. 0845 6060973. And on top of that, what was the thing for you that did work? I'll tell you what it is for me. Monday, my diet starts. For the simple reason that my daughter, last week, while messing about in the sitting room said: 'I've got a big fat tummy just like Dad!' And I thought something's got to give here, you know? I could end up being a big, bloated radio host and we've already got enough of them on this radio station so something's got to give. What's it going to be? What was it for you? What was the straw that broke the camel's back in your health regime, in your weight-related issues? And do we think that getting 450 pounds for losing 50 pounds is likely to work? The phone lines are wide open ... '

And there it is. Battle lines drawn. Enemy established. Phones ringing. Of course, I didn't realise at the time that I was deploying tropes that could be easily transferred into areas where I feel deep and sincere sympathy for the people being targeted, but it's clear now that I was.

In my defence – and I clearly need one – I was newish in the job and the radio phone-in is, traditionally, a medium that thrives, even depends, on turning us against each other. There was also that ever-present fear of silence, of the phones not ringing and of being left talking into the ether for hours. So, when I started out, I listened to other presenters and, while apparently disgusted by the way they talked about immigrants or Muslims or gypsies, I clearly absorbed at least some of their *modus operandi* by a sort of auditory osmosis. It's obviously not enough to claim that I attacked the obese in this way by accident or out of professional necessity, though. There is too much relish in my voice to get away with that, too much obvious enjoyment of the verbal fireworks I was lobbing at people to whom, despite the pleading emails and the occasional distraught caller, I barely gave a second thought.

I can remember quite clearly, and with a profound sense of shame, the precise moment at which the scales fell from my eyes. I almost wish it was a more complicated or sophisticated story because its very obviousness adds to my embarrassment. Though there is some comfort, perhaps, in the thought that it can be so easy to step away from wrongness in which you have previously revelled.

When my oldest daughter started school, we were in the lucky position of being able to hire someone to help with childcare. The woman we found, who remains beloved of both girls and a dear friend of our family, has struggled with her weight for her entire life. I don't mean weight-loss clubs and the bottles of low-calorie pop that were a fixture of our fridge when I was growing up as Mum, like most women of her generation, was always on one diet or another. I mean serious medical issues and bouts of crippling self-loathing. There is a gentleness to Maria, a fundamental kindness that is so rare we knew from the start that we had been very lucky to find her. And yet, when she came into our lives, I was still regularly lampooning 'fatty fatty fat fats' on a radio show that, it transpired, she usually enjoyed listening to with her dad.

So it seems somewhat pathetic to admit that all it took for me to recognise the base cruelty of my rhetoric was for the face of someone who cared for my children to pop into my head when I was about to embark on another 'hilarious' tirade. But it was. I'm not sure why but the epic inadequacy of trying to tell myself that I didn't mean *her* was suddenly and completely clear. Of course I meant her. And of course I meant the kind, patient email correspondent whom I wish I could apologise to directly today. And every other similarly poorly person for whom the instruction to 'eat less and exercise more' would be as useful as telling a Covid-19 patient to 'fight' their way to health. It really didn't matter what I thought I was doing or how I justified it. I was hurting people for no reason other than my own amusement and advancement. But I'm still no closer to understanding *why* I ended up in such an ugly place.

One of the single most illuminating experiences of my professional life came from discussions about the abduction of the three-year-old English girl Madeleine McCann from a

Portuguese holiday apartment in 2007 while her parents were dining with friends a few hundred yards away. I still reel at the memory of the vitriol and hate directed at those parents, Kate and Gerry, in the immediate aftermath of the tragedy and for years afterwards. On paper, you would think that a mother and a father enduring what is surely every parent's worst nightmare could at least depend upon public sympathy, but there was precious little for the McCanns.

I learned from my callers that it had been commonplace in British holiday camps for parents to tie a handkerchief to their chalet door so that passers-by could listen out for the crying of an unattended child within and report it. The compere at various onsite events would then announce that a child was crying in, say, chalet 47 and a parent would rush back. Yet much of the opprobrium directed at the McCanns hinged upon a widespread insistence that no decent holidaying parent would ever leave a child unattended. I wonder how many children of the seventies *didn't* get left alone by their parents on occasion. Mum and Dad once emerged from the dining room of a guest house in Morecambe to find me and my sister comfortably ensconced in the front row of the television lounge watching *Morecambe and Wise* with the assembled pensioners some two hours after they had put us to bed and headed downstairs for dinner. Nevertheless, people poured over maps of the resort, cast astonishing aspersions on the conduct of everybody present and, ultimately, argued that the parents must have harmed their own child and hidden the evidence.

The whole horrible business introduced to me the concept of anonymous online trolling, a subject on which I could probably write a PhD thesis these days. The internet was awash with people, their true identities always concealed, who dedicated astonishing amounts of time to trolling the McCanns: abusing, accusing, attacking. Some seven years after Madeline's disappearance, one of these so-called trolls was filmed but not named by Sky News. Days later, she tragically took her own life and I found myself grimly fascinated by the thought processes that had led her into such a dark and dangerous place.

Perhaps it is further evidence of my 'snowflake' status but I refuse to believe that most people who engage in horrible behaviour are inherently horrible people. Often, of course, they see themselves as crusaders for the truth or enemies of a malign 'Establishment' but I am more interested in how an outwardly ordinary individual can end up disseminating such extraordinary nastiness. Albeit on a less serious scale, I think the answer might also explain my own abuse of the obese.

No matter how hard we try to insulate ourselves from the vagaries of fortune, we know somewhere deep inside that we have very little control over the events that shape us. I love the Robert Burns poem about the best-laid plans of mice and men and, like all great art, it speaks to a universal truth. It doesn't matter how hard we strain to keep ourselves and our loved ones safe, that safety can never be fully guaranteed. Those plans 'gang aft agley'.

We see it in the relatively recent phenomenon of 'helicopter parenting', wrapping our children in so much metaphorical cotton wool that they can barely move. I think, though, that we do this more for our own peace of mind than from any exceptional concern for our children's safety. Galloping technology and our uniquely selfish times have conspired to create an environment in which we feel so discombobulated and fearful when we don't know where our children are that we track and restrict their movements more for our own mental equilibrium than for their actual security. I remember, when my daughters were very young, arguing on air that it was ridiculous to give schoolchildren mobile phones. When one dissenting father explained that he would know whether his son had been abducted, I arrogantly explained that the first thing any kidnapper would do is throw away his victim's phone. Nonetheless, when mine reached the same age they were kitted out with not just the phones but also the very latest tracking app.

To what purpose? To reassure me and their mum that, every time we checked their whereabouts, they were OK. It doesn't seem too much of a stretch to suggest that the next stage of this obviously flawed reasoning (you're not even checking on the whereabouts of your child, you're checking on the whereabouts of their phone) is to look askance at anyone to whom bad things actually have happened. If it is their fault that horror entered their life then it follows that you can control whether horror enters yours. So maligning the McCanns becomes a way in which we can provide ourselves with a false reassurance that it is our behaviour and not dumb, hateful luck that brings tragedy into our orbits. And the more furiously and publicly you attack them for their 'choices', the more reassured you will be that similar vicissitudes and horrors cannot arrive uninvited in your own life.

Somewhere deep inside, I have always wanted to be better-looking. Throughout my life, I have been cursed with handsome friends and I was always acutely conscious of where I sat in the hierarchy. When I was young, I was stick thin and so self-conscious about it that I regularly wore two jackets. As I grew older, I became flabby, pot-bellied and periodically possessed of what are generally known as 'man boobs'. Rather unfairly, now I come to think of it, I cannot actually recall a hiatus between these two conditions during which I was at anything like an optimum weight. My point here is that my comments about and attitude towards obese people were, I think now, more about me than them.

I knew that my own condition was a combination of laziness, alcohol and gluttony and I hated the fact that I didn't seem able to do anything about it. Rather than asking for help, then, I took to lashing out at people who reminded me of my own perceived failings and angrily insisting that obesity was entirely the responsibility of the individual. After all, if it wasn't the fault of the individual, if it wasn't a problem simply solved by telling people to 'eat less and exercise more', then I would have had to confront the reality of my own situation and acknowledge that I needed some support. This was just one

more area in which my 'stiff upper lip', my armour, my permanent hypervigilance simply couldn't admit vulnerability or suffering. To do so would be to tug on a thread that might unravel
my entire personality, so instead I attacked. 'Fat-shaming'
remains popular and it is notable that many of its most enthusiastic exponents are not exactly pictures of health or paragons
of self-care.

Hate, at its heart, is about the exercise of power. In my
experience, public hate usually involves the exercise of one,
unhealthy, type of power in an effort to disguise or deny the
absence of another, altogether healthier, type. The McCann
trolls exercised enormous but entirely malign power over the
suffering family but they did so to hide from the absence of
power they could exercise over their own lives. It is easy to
describe these people as lonely, bitter and twisted but I think
we all have a bit of this mindset lurking within us. They
attacked the McCanns as a way of denying their own impotence; I attacked obese people as a way of denying my own
inability or even refusal to better look after myself. A xeno-
phobe is someone who attacks people born somewhere else as
a way of denying that his own life has become so small and (in
his secret heart) worthless that he has to pretend a geographi-
cal accident is some sort of achievement. Moreover, he has to
hate everybody who didn't win the bogus jackpot in order to
shore up the notion that his 'prize' has any real value at all.

The abiding truth here is that we all lash out at others
because of pain we are nursing ourselves. And yet hurting

someone else, no matter how efficiently or frequently or 'amusingly' we may do it, will never take away our own pain. On a personal level, we can't change the world or the people around us through effort or force of will; all we can do is try to make changes to ourselves in the hope that the world around us will then respond differently to our presence in it. I'm not going to get healthier by attacking obese people. She's not going to get less scared by attacking Kate and Gerry McCann. He's not going to become more comfortable in his own skin by attacking the colour of somebody else's.

These days, I am able to see that life is defined by two forces: the external and the internal. We sometimes seem so completely conditioned to believe that our happiness depends upon external forces, over which we can exercise next to no control, that we forget not only that it is determined by the internal, but also that we can, with help and guidance, exercise some very real control over that. Next time you catch yourself criticising or mocking someone for some aspect of their existence over which they have little or no control, try asking yourself why *you* care about it. I never cease to be stunned by how often, when I try this simple exercise, I turn out to have no answer at all.

Chapter 7
TRANS

I DON'T REALLY WANT to write about transgenderism. Every time I poke my head above the parapet and try to frame my thoughts on the matter, it very nearly gets blown off by one 'side' or the other. On one side of the debate are those who believe trans people deserve the same rights and protections as everyone else and strive to raise awareness of the abuses suffered by this marginalised group. On the other sits a spectrum, ranging from women who fear that affording trans people the same rights as them might damage female equality; to those who are less comfortable with the very concept and would say they had a more 'traditional', binary view of gender; as well as those who actively and aggressively seek to persecute what they see as abnormality.

Worse, it is an area in which trying to build bridges between two passionately opposed positions invariably sees you coming under attack from both of them. At least it does when it's me. So that's why I don't really want to write about transgenderism. But I think that I should, for three reasons.

First, I know that my 'opinions' must be at least partly wrong because they so clearly and completely contradict each other. It would not be an exaggeration to say that when we discuss the issue on the radio show I can feel my position shifting from one caller to the next. Afterwards, I can somehow hold two ideas to be simultaneously true, despite knowing that they simply can't coexist in any plausible reality. As someone who delights in pointing out other people's cognitive dissonance, it seems only fair that I should own my own here.

Second, I don't ever want to be a person who stops *thinking* because they are cowed by criticism and I think I have come closer to that place with transgenderism than with any other subject. The abuse received by women, and some men, who insist upon the biological reality of womanhood is infinitely worse than the abuse heaped upon me by both their supporters and opponents. I am in no doubt of that. And it pales further in comparison to the abuse received by many in the transgender community itself, a third of whom, according to a 2018 Stonewall report, were discriminated against in public because of their gender identity in that year alone. But for my own part, it is still jarring and occasionally upsetting to be called, for example, misogynistic or transphobic by people who passionately believe that I am, however flimsy their evidence.

One of the most surreal experiences of my broadcasting career involved seeing the transcript of a call to the programme in response to my own experiences in shop changing rooms reproduced online by the caller with each of my comments and

questions to her followed by brackets in which, under the head-
ing 'subtext', she detailed what I had *really* meant by the words
I had used. I'm still not sure whether to admire or condemn the
audacity of someone who, if a conversation hasn't unfolded in a
way that they like, insists that the actual conversation never took
place at all and only they can explain what the *real*, unheard and
unspoken words were, but it took my breath away. I would say
now, cautiously, that such experiences are typical of much of the
debate surrounding this most vexed of issues.

So I will write here honestly and perhaps clumsily in the hope
that laying out my experiences, thoughts and feelings, and the processes behind them, deserves at least the courtesy of contempla-
tion. If I am 'wrong' then showing my working will allow you, and
possibly me, to identify precisely where mistakes have been made.
At the very least, I would hope to show that allowing well-meaning and honest people to make such mistakes is a prerequisite of
helping any of us ever change our minds about anything.

Third, and this is perhaps hardest to explain but easiest to
demonstrate, people possessed of truly vile and indefensible
opinions regarding race and sexuality are seeking, with much
success, to co-opt the trans debate. At its simplest, racists,
misogynists and homophobes claim that if you have any issues
with the idea of affording trans women exactly the same rights
as cisgender women (the prefix cis simply means 'on the same
side as', so cisgender people remain 'on the same side' of the
gender they were initially identified as at birth) then you're on
the same side as them in a mostly mythical 'culture war'. People

who actually want to assign rights according to ethnicity or nationality, sex or even sexuality point to attempts to 'silence' people who question whether trans women can or should enjoy all rights afforded to cisgender women and claim a bogus and cynical allegiance. This notion of 'culture war', incidentally, is mostly the latest incarnation of 'political correctness gone mad', where people dishonestly claim they are somehow 'not allowed' to say what they want to say. It is, as usual, criticism and evidence-based condemnation that they are really objecting to. If you were to attack, say, the Duchess of Sussex, Meghan Markle, much more frequently and viciously than her sister-in-law, the Duchess of Cambridge – even for things that both women have done – then pointing out that there is probably a racial subtext to your condemnations is, in this context, supposedly calling for you to be 'cancelled' and being unforgivably 'woke' (conscious of systemic inequality). By way of example, both women had lily-of-the-valley in their wedding bouquets but one British tabloid published the headline: 'How Meghan Markle's Flowers May Have Put Princess Charlotte's Life at Risk'.

The sort of people who call for 'uppity' women of colour to know their place or for homosexuals, refugees or Muslims to be 'cured', punished or marginalised from the rest of the population have, without most of us noticing, successfully hitched themselves to the so-called 'anti-trans' movement in a way that is explicitly designed to conflate these issues. So when I explain that there is mostly no such thing as a 'culture war', it is generally people in one, two, three or all of these categories that prove most desperate to argue that there is. And when you look at the tactics deployed by people who want to deny any space at all for questioning the notion that trans women should be treated *identically* to cis women in any conceivable scenario, it's hard to escape the conclusion that they accidentally nurtured this disingenuous and dangerous conflation themselves.

So it is that, in the dishonest and rather dirty hands of professional hate-mongers, the attempted silencing or 'cancelling' of so-called 'transphobes' on college campuses and elsewhere becomes proof that they are also being unfairly attacked for entirely different and altogether more obnoxious 'opinions'. 'There is no culture war,' a well-meaning liberal might say. 'Yes there is,' screams a sexist, Donald Trump-supporting, racism-denying, Muslim-hating, homophobic sad sack in response. 'Just look at the way "they" treat women who just don't want to share their toilets with people who have penises.' And on top of that, to my profound shock and continuing confusion, are the female academics insisting there absolutely is a 'culture war' underway because people unsuccessfully tried to get them sacked simply for stating that 'biological sex is real'. I trust you can already see what I meant about unintentionally upsetting everybody every time I even try to articulate thoughts on this topic?

Let's begin with the cognitive dissonance. As a heterosexual man, with nearly 50 years on this earth, it currently seems to me to be perfectly reasonable to suggest that human beings in possession of a penis should not be allowed in to 'female only' spaces. Women who worry that it is too easy for men to 'self-identity' as women in order to gain access to 'female only' areas for nefarious or voyeuristic reasons seem to me to be completely deserving of my support and understanding. And I can sustain and argue this position right up to the point that a trans woman asks who will be inspecting the contents of her underwear to determine whether or not she is permitted entry. The British model, writer and trans activist Paris Lees pointed out to me that she has been exclusively using 'female only' facilities for almost all of her adult life without issue, and that I have enjoyed her company on various occasions without knowing or caring whether or not she possesses a penis.

Can you, on this evidence, pick a 'side' here? Can you tell that trans woman to show you – or the underpants police – her genitalia before she can continue using the only facilities she's used for years? Or would you tell a woman to ignore her fears and concerns about being assaulted or raped or spied upon and open the changing room door to anyone who wants to come through it as long as they tick a box marked 'I'm a woman' on the way in? I just can't, and the weirdest thing about the whole debate is that there are people on both 'sides' who will despise you for your inability to see this issue as clearly as they apparently do.

My head tells me that the incidences of men maliciously infiltrating female-only spaces by classifying themselves as women are rare enough to be negligible and that the experiences in other countries where such equality of access is enshrined in law do not offer up any major grounds for concern. My heart, however, tells me that essentially ordering countless deeply uncomfortable women to do something that causes them real and considerable distress is fundamentally wrong. I once naively thought that cubicles and partitions might provide a solution to the impasse but they simply protect cis women from catching an accidental glimpse of a trans woman's penis. They do not protect them in any way from the attentions of a man who has entered their space dishonestly.

One of the writers I find most persuasive and challenging on this issue explained to me that simply knowing that there are no male eyes present in a clothes shop dressing room is a uniquely liberating experience. She told me that something as simple as removing her bra in order to try on a strapless dress would become fraught with worry unless she can be as confident as possible that the only people present are women. This seemed eminently reasonable to me at the time and still does. I don't think many men understand the constant threat of unwanted attention and male violence that women live with as a matter of course. The #MeToo movement has proved something of a turning point but the road ahead is still incredibly long. It wasn't always the case, but I can't currently see 'female spaces' meaning much unless it is in the context of this constant threat.

And then, just as I think I've managed to reach a consistent position, I'm asked the question about underwear examinations again. What if the woman in the next cubicle is a pre-op transsexual? Perhaps she doesn't want to have the op at all but would be at least as disturbed as my friend by the thought of a man spying on her when she took off her bra. Where should she go to try on a strapless dress? You see now, I hope, why I think it's so important that we be allowed to be confused. And we haven't even touched upon the quiddity of womanhood or the (im)possibility of changing 'sex' as opposed to gender. Never mind the fact that I'm a man and so arguably sticking my nose into things that don't concern me.

It was, in retrospect, not entirely helpful that my first guide through this minefield was a trans man. He was brilliant and bright, and persuaded me within moments of meeting that he had absolutely spent his childhood trapped in a body he did not want or recognise as his own. I was deeply moved by the whole experience but worry now that it blinded me to the very different problems generated by the opposite transformation.

It was also, in retrospect, not as relevant as I thought that I used to accompany my daughters, with permission, into cubicles in shop changing rooms when they were younger because they liked shopping for clothes with their dad. I like to think that this was due to my eye for fashion but it was probably because I'm a softer touch than their mum and so more likely to let them buy both outfits instead of insisting that they choose just one. They're older now and probably can't imagine anything worse than going clothes shopping with me but these are really happy memories for me. Until recently, I was baffled by the notion that there was something so wrong with *me* being in *there*.

I wrote at length in my last book about Lucy Meadows, a trans woman teacher who took her own life after an almost unbelievable campaign of media vilification initiated by the *Daily*

Mail columnist Richard Littlejohn. I think her memory also affects my objectivity. Finding ways to avoid having to watch other people being pushed down a similar path seems crucial, but I'm no longer sure it can be prioritised so completely that all other concerns and considerations are crowded out of the conversation. It is, in other words, easy to see the tragic results of divisive, bigoted commentators throwing ever more red meat of outrage at their readers and listeners and conclude that they are the only 'opposing' voices in the whole debate. Unfortunately, the lazy othering perpetrated by paid provocateurs who move seamlessly from trans women today to black men or unemployed people or single mothers tomorrow can't be ignored. For desiccated old men furious that they are no longer able to use the n-word, keep their wives on a financial leash or hurl abuse at gay men in the street, the trans community represents the last bastion of entirely innocent fellow humans they are currently permitted to publicly abuse with impunity. If nothing else, the fraudulent simplicity of their position does a grave disservice to the nuances and complexities of the broader debate. It took me a while to understand but focusing on them and their spurious arguments ultimately helps nobody. Let me show you what I mean.

In May of 2019, the then Work and Pensions Secretary Amber Rudd expressed the view that candidates in the unfolding Conservative Party leadership election should not 'parade' their wives in public because she was more 'interested in policies'. This proved to be a surprisingly controversial contention for some corners of the British media and many of my callers.

It prompted me to recall a couple of things regarding women's rights in the UK that, to my shame, I had only discovered while researching my last book. It's fair to say that Andy in Blackburn was unimpressed.

Andy: I just think the way you liberals speak is unbelievable. The nerve of you guys is unbelievable. I think this is a great thing. In today's age it's like you've got the bubonic plague if you promote traditional family values.

James: What do you mean by traditional family values?

Andy: The way you were speaking about it. Like it's a perverse thing that they've got these wives ...

James: No, what does it mean to you? What does the phrase 'traditional family values' mean to you?

Andy: Everything until people like you ruined it.

James: That's not really an answer. What is a traditional family value that you feel is no longer respected?

Andy: Well, erm, everything ...

James: Because the stuff I mentioned, if you're going to insist on using me as a lens through which to examine this issue, the stuff I mentioned was it being impossible in law to rape your own wife until the 1980s and it being impossible for women until the 1970s to get credit or a mortgage without having their brothers, husbands or fathers act as guarantors. They're the only two examples [of social change] that I gave. I'm going to give you a break here and suggest that you're not cross that this has changed, are you?

Andy: Who's advocating for that?

James: Exactly. But these are the only values I've mentioned today so I'm wondering which ones you refer to when you talk about traditional family values. Which ones did *you* mean?

Andy: I think feminism has made women miserable.

James: (unfairly, but give me a break here) I'm sure that most of the women you meet very quickly seem miserable but the question isn't about that. The question is, 'What are the values that you are here to support?'

Andy: (pause) I think it's pretty obvious.

James: Well, it's not obvious to me, Andy, which is why I've asked you 17 times!

Andy: OK. Traditional marriage. Having a mother and a father. The nuclear family. The 1950s and 60s.

James: So you feel that the nuclear family is under threat?

Andy: I think it's been denigrated.

James: By whom?

Andy: By the way you started off this entire subject by making it seem like this ['parading' of wives] is a perverse and strange thing.

James: So me, my wife, who I married in church, and our two children are representative of an assault upon family values? Just talk me through that.

Andy: You're twisting my words now.

James: OK. So can you name some traditional values that you think don't exist any more? Because Andy, mate, I'm beginning to think that you don't really know what you're cross about.

Andy: No, I do. I do. I'll tell you now. I think social engineering is going on and the way things are portrayed on the TV and the radio are the opposite of what they [traditional family values] are.

James: But you just need to give me some examples of the traditional values that you feel are somehow under siege. You haven't mentioned one yet.

Andy: By portraying them as somehow old-fashioned. That's what I'm saying.

James: (performatively frustrated) Portraying *what* as old-fashioned?

Andy: The nuclear family, for God's sake. How many times do I have to say it?

James: How is it being portrayed as old-fashioned? I'm in one!

Andy: But I'm saying that everything on the media these days, if it's not trans ...

James: Andy, you are literally on the media right now. No one's mentioned trans except you.

Andy: I'm talking about movies. Movies.

James: So which movies have been ruined by having too many trans people in them?

Andy: I'm not saying they've been ruined. I'm saying that, for such a tiny minority, they are massively over-represented in movies.

James: Which movies?

Andy: I'm not specifically ... I'm saying that you can't turn on the radio ...

James: Alright. Name a TV show, then.

Andy: I don't watch TV. I'm saying they [trans people] are over-represented.

James: *Mrs Doubtfire*? Is that what we're talking about?

Andy: You mean the Robin Williams movie?

James: Yes.

Andy: I wasn't specifically thinking of that, no.

James: But is the movie part of the assault on traditional family values?

Andy: I wouldn't say so, no.

James: So give me some examples of one that is.

Andy: Well, I wouldn't want to watch them.

James: But you're furious about the things you don't know, can't name and haven't watched?

Andy: I'm not furious. I'm not furious.

James: OK. So shall we have one more go at the traditional family values you feel are being somehow undermined?

Andy: I think they're portrayed as old-fashioned and out of place and as if you've got some sort of disease if you want to retain that.

James: And when I ask you for examples you say you don't know because you haven't seen any but you know that they're out there and they're awful.

Andy: Just turn on Sky TV.

James: I've got it on now in the studio.

Andy: MTV. You name it. You know exactly what I'm talking about. Social and cultural engineering is portraying a tiny minority as being in the majority and they're not.

James: (somewhat impatient now) Of what? A tiny minority of what?

Andy: Gay people. Trans people. People who want to marry their sisters.

James: People who want to marry their sisters?

Andy: I was in a cafe the other day and there was a woman saying that we used to think that gay marriage was a big no-no but it's not now so should we still feel upset towards brothers and sisters getting married? There's loads of YouTube videos featuring millennials who don't have a problem with it.

'Liberals'; 'millennials'; 'social engineering'; 'family values'; 'YouTube'. It's like a bingo card, isn't it? It was a few months before 'woke' and 'culture war' became popular in the UK but you can be fairly confident that Andy will have signed up to those by now as well.

Many people argue that in 50 years, or 20 or even 10, the trans debate today will seem as inappropriate and misguided as debates from yesterday about the reality of homosexuality or the acceptability of everything from equal marriage to apartheid. I know I was staggered to see a front cover of *Newsweek* magazine from 1995 that bore the enormous headline: 'Bisexuality', and beneath it: 'Not Gay. Not Straight. A New Sexual Identity Emerges.' But people like Andy, and more pertinently the professional purveyors of fact-free fury that he follows, led me to a place where I thought that these conversations were *already* of a piece. Because some of the bigotry displayed towards trans people is *outwardly* identical to the bigotry directed at other vulnerable communities, I think I presumed that the motivations of all people that we might call trans-sceptic were the same as the usual motivations of common or garden bigots. This, obviously, is exactly what the people who filled Andy's head with nonsense want us *all* to think – that trans issues are just another nail in the coffin of unspecified 'traditional family values' already battered by every single step towards any concept of 'equal rights'. If you want women to know their place, people of colour to stay in their lane, gays to hide away and certainly not entertain ludicrous notions of getting married, or people from other countries to go back to them, then the whole trans debate is a gift-wrapped invitation to explain how *everybody* opposed to you is an echo-chamber-dwelling, ultra-woke, social-justice warrior who can't stop virtue signalling and wants to chase everyone who disagrees with them out of their jobs and homes.

It may be that arguments about trans women's continuing access to 'female only' spaces do end up looking like arguments about racial segregation or the criminalisation of homosexuality in years to come. I simply don't know. But they don't look like that at the moment and, unless we are permitted to be publicly and politely 'wrong' on the issue, the debate will continue to be co-opted by all the 'culture war' fraudsters who are becoming increasingly bold in their demands to be free from *all* scrutiny and criticism. It seems essential and urgent that we separate the trans debate from all the other areas of social policy where, to borrow a phrase, equality can feel like oppression to people who have always been privileged. Having come under concerted attack from people allied with both 'sides' of this argument, I can state with some confidence that they all need to turn away from everyone using the issue to draw attention to themselves and instead try talking more to each other. This would also open up space for those us unallied with either to do more thinking in public.

The next call, I hope, demonstrates the importance and perhaps the current impossibility of us all having these conversations in the way that I believe we need to. The space and time available also, perhaps, highlights the futility of trying to do things like this on social media. The more vexed the issue the more I value contributors like Jane. I ask them questions not to try to trip them up (although I obviously do plenty of that in other contexts) but in the hope that their certainty might somehow rub off on me. I really wish I could see things as clearly and simply as she does. This call followed comments from the author J.K. Rowling about the impossibility of changing sex as opposed to gender. Rowling tweeted:

Dress however you please.
Call yourself whatever you like.
Sleep with any consenting adult who'll have you.
Live your best life in peace and security.
But force women out of their jobs for stating that sex is real?
#IStandWithMaya #ThisIsNotADrill

Maya here is Maya Forstater, who lost her job at an international thinktank after a series of tweets, including one in which she said: 'Men cannot change into women.' Again, at first glance I agree with this. At second glance, I realise I don't agree with it enough to argue the point with a trans friend or colleague. This is, I realise, unsatisfactory but it is also honest and, I think, human.

Jane: Women are being very kind. We are saying that trans women are women. OK. That's fine. But we have to draw the line and biology is the line and I'm so glad J.K. Rowling has helped us draw that line. Because we're oppressed because of our biology.

James: Yes.

Jane: Women around the world are oppressed because they are biologically women. We're not oppressed because of the dresses we wear. It's nothing to do with what we look like on the outside.

James: (maybe trying a bit too hard to show that I 'get' it) You're talking about physical attributes. You're talking about nine-month gestation periods. You're talking about responsibility for children regardless of the circumstances which caused the pregnancy ...

Jane: I'm talking about female genital mutilation. I'm talking about being raped. Trans women don't suffer from female genital mutilation. That is suffered by females. Trans women aren't raped like women are. Trans women aren't murdered twice a week by their partners. This is all happening to females. Women need to be able to say, 'We are oppressed by the oppressor class, who are male.' And we can't talk about our axis of oppression if we no longer own that word. We will say 'women'. We will be kind. We will say trans women are women.

James: But it's the identicalness, for want of a better word, that you object to? You cannot be identical.

Jane: (laughing) You know it's not true, James. The world knows it's not true.

James: I know what's not true?

Jane: Females don't have penises. You know, people will bring up things called disordered sexual ...

James: I'm sorry. Please don't take this the wrong way but you're talking too quickly and I'm struggling to keep up.

Jane: I'm sorry. I'm nervous. After we last spoke, I had to delete my social media I was so afraid.

James: (churlishly and unhelpfully) 'Well, welcome to my world. (Jane laughs.)

But don't tell me what I think or what I know when I'm asking you questions designed to fill gaps in my knowledge and my understanding because that's not helpful. And it's not true. I won't ask you questions that I know the answer to.

Jane: OK.

James: So how is it about more than words?

Jane: How is it about more than words? It's biology.

James: But that's a word.

Jane: (laughs) OK. Woman is not a feeling in a man's head. We have been commoditised.

James: So you don't recognise 'trans' in any way then? There's no such thing as 'trans' because if you were born in *that body* ...

Jane: Of course I believe that there are trans women.

James: So what feeling have they got in their head?

Jane: They think they are women.

James: Right.

Jane: But that does not make them biologically female.

James: So it's about the word 'biologically', which the last caller said we misuse.

Jane: How can it be wrong to say that women are adult human females? How can that be wrong?

James: I don't know. That's one of the things I'm trying to find out. Can we be a bit reductionist? If it's biology then it is organs and genitalia. Do you cease to be a woman if, say, you have no ovaries or you don't menstruate?

Jane: (laughing) No!

James: Why not?

Jane: Why not? OK. Female is down to whether you can produce large gametes that are immobile.

James: I'm sorry, I don't know what that means.

Jane: It's sperm or ova. Was your body built to be able to produce them?

James: You know there are lots of people who were born infertile?

I am, for the record, very close to being one of them myself. Without the appliance of science it is almost impossible that I could have fathered my own biological children.

Given the reasons we suspect lay behind my mum's failure to conceive, this raises the very real possibility of my dad and I being the world's only recorded case of hereditary male infertility. Sort of.

Jane: Yes, but their body was built to be able to do it. However, the fact they can't do it doesn't stop them being of the sex that was built to be able to do it.

James: Do you see why that sounds a little bit complicated? The idea that biology is defined by reproductive potential?

Jane: How else is it defined?

James: I don't know. I'm asking you.

Jane: Even asparagus is defined by ...

James: So an infertile woman is less of a woman than a fertile woman.

Jane: No. Because she was built to be able to produce the large gametes.

James: But what does that mean if she can't do it? You're calling her defective.

Jane: (laughs) She would probably call herself defective.

James: (who has received fertility treatment, remember) Well we'd have to ask her and I'm not sure she'd thank us for laughing at the idea. So if you're talking about gradations of womanhood ...

Jane: No, I'm not. *You're* talking about gradations of womanhood. I'm talking about the females being the people who are able, hopefully, to produce live young.

James: And if they can't?

Jane: And if they can't they are still built to be able to produce live young. And they are oppressed.

James: That doesn't really work for me, Jane.

Jane: (laughing) OK. What's the difference between you and your daughters?

James: Um. In what context?

Jane: You know what I mean.

James: OK. They're girls and I'm a man?

Jane: And what will they grow up to be?

James: I don't know.

This may look glib on my part but it really isn't. I would defy anyone who has spoken in depth with the parent of a trans child – and I have spoken with many – to see the question Jane just asked me as being as simple and straightforward as she sincerely believes it to be. It also seems relevant to mention that I never feel more behind the times or out of touch with social progress than when I hear my daughters' generation discussing gender, sex and sexuality. It is a generalisation, of course, and a criticism of neither constituency to say that they are almost entirely unfazed by the things that continue to confound many of their elders.

Jane: Well, they will grow up to be oppressed because they are female. They will be paid less because they are female.

James: Why have we moved away from reproduction? If they grow up and can't have babies they will still be women.

Jane: Exactly. There you go.

James: And yet there's someone else over there who can't have babies and you're saying they're not women.

Jane: Because they were built to produce sperm.

James: And then they've had an operation to prevent them from ever doing that again?

Jane: 97 per cent of trans women ...

James: I'm not interested. I'm talking about the example I'm using to examine the philosophy that we're discussing.

Jane: So the 3 per cent of women who fully transition are trans women and women are being very kind and saying you can say that trans women are women. But 90 per cent of trans women do not have any surgery.

James: So what's the difference between them, then?

Jane: Penises.

James: Right.

Jane: But their biology's still the same and there are plenty of trans women out there who would say, 'Yes, I'm male. I fathered three children.'

James: And you're alright with them?

Jane: I'm alright with anybody who believes in biology.

James: Where our definition of biology is being built in a way to do something without it mattering whether you can actually do it or not? So how do we define biological womanhood? It means you were built in a way that allows you to produce eggs and give birth. Except hundreds of thousands of women can't. But they're still women because maybe if the dice had rolled differently they could have done. I think the trans [woman's] argument would be, well, the dice did roll very differently for me, and I can't do that, but I am a woman. So that's the bit I struggle with.

And I still do. It's not hard to feel the intuitive good sense of what Jane said but my questions were honest and, for me at least, 'biology' takes us some way short of where we need to get to for the debate to be over. I also still hear vague echoes here of claims made about homosexuality being somehow 'unnatural' because there is no prospect of procreation. I stress, for the umpteenth time, that I have these conversations and write these words because I don't see how the current furious impasse will ever be breached if neither 'side' wants the other even to be heard.

At the risk of leaving you in as much of a tailspin as I find myself whenever this subject comes up, here is a caller who comes at the issue from an altogether different perspective. Tony rang to join the discussion about reports that ten-year-old children were being asked to answer the following question by the NHS: 'Do you feel the same inside as the gender you were born with? (feeling male or female)'. Had I been in charge I might have also asked the ten-year-olds whether or not they found the original question in any way hard to understand or answer. Tony is talking about his own child. I don't think you get calls like his or Jane's if the people listening to the programme don't believe they can *trust* the presenter. As I get older, this seems to me to be more important than the question of whether or not we *agree*. Where once I would use callers to burnish my own certainties, today I prefer to dig deep into their arguments in the hope of illuminating the issue for listeners. Tony rang me two years before Jane and I think you can probably see some of my own struggles with the issues reflected in a comparison of the two calls.

Tony: He's on hormonal treatment. Only two weeks ago he's been up to Harley Street and had his nose worked on to make him look more feminine. Or *her* look more feminine. It's very difficult to talk about him or her. I don't really know what to say.

James: Nor do I. What does your child say?

Tony: Well, he doesn't seem to know where to stop. This is what's upsetting us, you know. He's going to have his Adam's apple looked at because that will higher his voice but when he is (pause) my daughter or our daughter, he speaks, she speaks really feminine. The transition is unbelievable. I mean people say 'transgender' or, you know, 'cross dresser'. It's nothing like that. Some days he just feels more comfortable as a male and another day, you know, he just wants to be female. It depends on the situation and whether or not he's got to go to work. I mean, he runs an office up in London.

James: Well, it's the denial, the repression that causes the problems, I think. It doesn't necessarily mean that he wants to run around dressed like Bet Lynch every day, he just wants to be free to put on the outside what he's feeling on the inside every day. Is that right?

Tony: I've been out with her for meals and things.

James: You're an amazing man, Tony. Can I ask how old you are?

Tony: Well, I'm 73.

James: So you weren't expecting to be dealing with this in the autumn of your years?

Tony: (chuckling) I thought I'd experienced everything in life but nothing like that, believe me.

James: Can I ask about your wife? Because you mentioned that she's not finding it as easy as you are and most people listening will completely sympathise with that position.

Tony: She can't come to terms with it. She hasn't yet seen ... (pause) ... her.

James: Yes.

Tony: She ... she understands ... she says 'I support you', you know, but she can't physically see him in the flesh, or her in the flesh. And I feel she's missing out on so much because (heavy sigh) ... I just wish she would come out with us. I mean, the whole family knows. I mean, we've told everyone in the close family. We've got everyone's full support. You know, I've shown them photographs. I walk around with photographs and everyone is amazed, you know.

James: Tony, your family is this entire issue in microcosm. Your daughter struggled ... Or rather your son struggled until he became your daughter at which point you managed to move with it – as I am trying to do as a member of this society without any personal investment – your wife *can't* move with it just like lots of other members of society who don't have a child with gender dysphoria. You've got almost every angle covered. And I can hear the sadness in your voice about the fracture that's still there.

Tony: Well, that is the sad side of it, really. Because I feel that as a mother she's missed all this and having brought him up as a son – obviously she had more dealings with him than I did – and yet she's missed this. To suddenly put [the past] in a box and open up another one ...

James: Is she cross or sad or confused or all of the above?

Tony: We cannot really discuss it without, you know, a bit of hysterics coming in. I think we should all talk about it and go to see, you know, people who can help with the situation but it's got to come from within. I'm just hoping that one day we'll all be sorted and we can be one big, happy family.

James: There's a lot of love coming into this studio for you, Tony, and that's why I do what I do. In the hope that, whatever the subject, someone who's just *living it* will give the rest of us a quick steer on whatever we're banging on about and why.

Tony: It's nothing to be frightened of. Just go with the flow and try to understand. As long as everyone's happy. That's what we're looking for.

One day, Tony, one day ...

Chapter 8

CONFESSIONS OF A CORPSE-MUNCHING PSYCHOPATH

WHEN I STARTED WRITING this book, I wondered if the reasons why I had come to be wrong about trivial things were similar, or the same, as those that had brought me to the wrong conclusions about more serious matters. Could the palpably absurd opinions I held about, say, tattoos or vegetarians be the result of the same processes that once led me to be supportive of teachers beating children in their care or the police racially profiling stop and search victims? I was wary of this thought, though, because I worried that comparing the *processes* would bestow some sort of equivalence upon the *results*. But actually, I don't think it does. I've realised that the experiences and reactions which lead us to wrongness about the silly stuff are just less profound versions of the experiences and reactions that lead us to being wrong about the deadly serious.

The phrase 'childhood trauma', for example, can be used to describe the encounter with 'Spiderman' at my mum's make-up counter just as accurately as it can the violence visited upon me by my old headmaster or even the unthinkable abuses endured by my old schoolmates and children everywhere. Similarly, screwing down emotional pain or 'manning up' not just to survive boarding schools but to actively flourish in them is, obviously, a far more preferable experience than 'manning up' to survive and actively flourish in a culture of criminal gangs. As I hope is clear, I'm certainly not conflating the two. It is the process that is the same.

It seems to me that the things that prevent us from feeling proper empathy towards people with very different life experiences – of understanding the negative experiences that contributed to making *them* who *they* are – are born of an ongoing failure and reluctance to address the negative experiences that contributed to making *us* who *we* are. 'It didn't do me any harm' was a lie I told myself to try to make it all OK, and in denying what happened to me I was able to deny the power something similar has to hurt others.

I hope that by showing how these experiences from my schooldays led me to various places I am delighted and relieved to be now moving away from, I may have made it easier to understand how much more serious traumas play a part in producing much more emotionally crippled adults. The point, of course, is that although some of us suffer much less pain than others, the condition itself is treatable.

*

The shadow of the Covid-19 virus has loomed large over everything in 2020, this book being no exception. Oddly, if I had not been convinced of the utter unfitness of Donald Trump and Boris Johnson for high office I may not have been able to write it at all. Without the abject madness of Brexit and the ensuing march to power of these two men, I would likely not have felt an urgent duty to shout the truth about Johnson and Trump from the rooftops and so wouldn't have given up presenting duties on the BBC, which demands scrupulous impartiality and would have prevented me from expressing any political opinions publicly. To see my warnings about their incompetence and moral decrepitude so completely validated by their responses to the pandemic has been horrible, of course. Rather predictable has been the enduring inability of many of their supporters to admit this to themselves, even as Trump moved from calling the virus a 'hoax' to promoting bleach as a possible treatment and Johnson, who went on holiday at the beginning of the outbreak, described his own presiding over one of the worst death rates in the world as a 'great success'.

Funnily enough, I voted for Boris Johnson to be mayor of London in 2008. Seen through the lens of the 'footballification' of politics – of bolting on your team's bobble hat and seeking to undermine anything the other side says, regardless of its value – there are two ways of interpreting this. It is either conclusive proof that I am a secret supporter of the cronyism, dishonesty and carnage that typified Johnson's first year as prime minister or, if you're on the other 'team', it demonstrates that *all* of my opinions and convictions are worthless because anyone who ends up believing the polar opposite of what they did a decade ago is clearly utterly unreliable and probably lying. Furthermore, as someone who also strained to remain clear-eyed about his rival for the premiership, Jeremy Corbyn, I bear personal responsibility for Johnson's election in 2019. This fetishisation of stubbornness practised by both camps continues to astound me even as I come closer to understanding how and why it happens. We can't change the way the world responds to our own admissions of wrongness but we can change the way we feel about making them.

I voted for Boris Johnson to be mayor of London because I wasn't very politically engaged or informed at the time; I thought he was likeable and funny on the TV and I was unforgivably relaxed about his well-established penchant for mocking and insulting ethnic minorities. I also somehow managed to overlook my own rather strict attitudes to morality and family values and give him a free pass for his sexual incontinence and serial philandering. Ten years later, of course, almost the entire Conservative party would do exactly the same and somehow manage to swallow down decades of professing to care passionately about things like fidelity, family and personal responsibility. On a personal level, this is tough enough to admit, on a professional level it's close to a dereliction of duty. But I did it. I admit it. I regret it.

I wonder now whether some of the opprobrium we reserve for people who change their minds about politics and politicians springs from a suppressed knowledge that our own convictions are built on altogether flimsier foundations than we care to admit. And that if we were to expose them to similar scrutiny, we would inflict serious structural damage. The current trend in public discourse that continues to worry me most is the growing support for the idea that asking someone to explain their views is somehow the same as seeking to prevent them from expressing those views. If I have become an expert at anything, it is unpicking the false (or at least utterly unprovable) 'certainties' with which we all sometimes insulate ourselves from the myriad confusions of life. Calling people politely opposed to the demonstrable lunacy of Brexit 'traitors' or 'enemies of the people' is the result of precisely the same delusional desperation for certainty that also sees us burn each other at the stake for the 'sin' of believing in a slightly different brand of the same religion. I'm not saying these things are the same, just that the internal processes that get us to these points are similar.

Around the time that I voted for Boris Johnson, I was also carving out a niche as a passionate opponent of press regulation, albeit because of my ability to argue the toss in a studio as opposed to any particular newspaper pedigree. I remember finding myself on the same TV panel as Alastair Campbell, Tony Blair's famously gruff (some would use a stronger term) former director of communications. We were the bookends, with two other guests between us, on a stage in front of a TV studio audience and we were furiously opposed to each other. I was adamant that press regulation of any kind was a baby step towards a totalitarian state; he was equally persuaded that British newspapers had become Augean stables of misinformation and corrupt practices. He was right, of course. And I was wrong.

Phone-hacking, the blatant lies about European Union membership, the cynical and deliberate stoking of racial tensions, Hillsborough, the demonisation of immigrants and refugees, the destruction of lives like Lucy Meadows' ... I could, and often do, go on. In much the same way that people are desperate to conflate 'free speech' with 'freedom from scrutiny', so a 'free press' has come to mean leaving proprietors like Rupert Murdoch and the Barclay brothers 'free' to publish whatever they please without any real concern for either accuracy or the lives of their readers. To the continuing confusion of self-styled 'libertarians', many of our most valuable freedoms are delivered and protected by laws, yet since Murdoch bought the *Sun* in 1969, the entire industry has been descending into lawlessness. Incredible, really, to reflect now upon the fact that he was only permitted to make the purchase after promising the sellers, IPC, that he would publish a 'straightforward, honest newspaper' which would continue to support Labour. I'm not the man to determine precisely what form regulation should take but it clearly needs to depend upon much more than the whims and ambitions of billionaire, often tax-avoiding proprietors. Murdoch's first editor, incidentally, later declared that the release of Nelson Mandela from prison would be 'a crass error'. Today, his successors seek to denigrate Black Lives Matter and publish articles stating that 'We Need Less Islam'. *Plus ça change.*

Campbell's newspaper career was far more illustrious than mine but by the time of our odd encounter he had been in favour of greater regulation for years. I was, I can easily see now, acting out of a tribal loyalty that was quite blind. In my heart, I felt I was defending my journalist father, my journalist wife, my journalist friends. I thought I was upholding noble principles of public trust and speaking truth to power and that newspapers were a bulwark against oppressive government and political corruption. I often describe the victims of 'footballification' as having their tribal scarves tied so tightly around their throats that they impede the flow of oxygen to their brains. The description fits me perfectly here.

As I write, Boris Johnson has just put a newspaper owner and the son of a former KGB colonel in the House of Lords and nobody appears to know why. In the same week, Nigel Farage, that doughty champion of British freedom and independence, appeared in a BBC documentary about Rupert Murdoch. When he thought filming had stopped, he revealed that he had sought Murdoch's *permission* to contribute to the programme. The national narrative, as set by these right-wing newspapers, currently contemplates the defunding or even the closure of the institutionally unbiased BBC. It's not hard to join the dots.

But it is hard to join them when you feel that you have skin in the game. Many of my friends and former colleagues on Fleet Street, men and women whom I love and respect, remain as blind as I was to the harm we do to the country when we contribute to the commoditisation of hatred and inchoate anger that some of our newspapers represent. When you are complicit in the publication of untruths, designed to enrich your employer as people pay more to be terrified and enraged, it is easiest to persuade yourself that they are not untruths at all. A large number of these journalists of my acquaintance have persuaded themselves that the BBC is in need of radical reform. I think we have become so completely inured to the tyranny of right and, these days, far-right talking points that we have come to see the neutral middle as the 'left'.

Think of a picture on a wall. If your nose is pressed up against it you will struggle to see what it depicts. Take a few steps back and all becomes clear. That's why Alastair Campbell could see what had become of a profession we had both loved and joined with the best of intentions while I, at that time, could not. Incidentally, the body language in the studio displays much of what I have explored here. By the end we are mirror images of each other, snarling and rolling our eyes. The fists are up, the armour is on and the adrenaline is coursing through my veins. I landed some proper blows on this biggest of political beasts and, afterwards, I was delighted with myself. I was wrong, though. I was completely and horribly wrong. I reached that realisation long before I discovered that a

208

journalist on my late father's old newspaper, now owned by the Barclay brothers, was contacting former colleagues of mine in the vain hope of digging up 'dirt'. I was glad that he wasn't alive to witness it.

There are, however, circumstances in which I think this unthinking, unexamined, unearned loyalty makes sense, and understanding this involves a level of empathy I find hard to achieve. Years before the British Labour Party was polluted by base anti-Semitism at almost every level I was, I think, guilty of some similar transgressions. With precious little knowledge of the detail or the history, I would blithely launch into phone-ins about the brutality of Israeli foreign policy and reel furiously from the accusations of anti-Semitism that would always ensue. For years, I simply couldn't see how condemning a political action in a foreign country could possibly be mistaken for hatred of an entire people. And then I started listening more carefully to my callers.

The Jewish experience of persecution, like the black experience of slavery, is so visceral and embedded in their contemporary consciousness that those of us on the outside can barely conceive of its importance. I was born in 1972. That's *27 years* after the end of the Second World War in Europe. The number of years between my birth and today is almost double the number between my birth and the end of the Nazi Holocaust. And yet, for me and so many others, the Holocaust was more history book than lived experience. Even, if I'm honest, ancient history. It felt like something from the dim and distant past, perpetrated by people from almost a different species than my own. I could attack people who wondered why, when slavery was abolished so many years ago, people are still talking about it today, but it took me years to see the Holocaust and the state of Israel in the same light. The comedian and writer David Baddiel put it best when he told me, quite correctly, that his atheism would count for nothing if the Gestapo came calling. An accident of birth would sign his death warrant just as accidents of birth consigned generations of black men and women to slavery. Anti-Semitism is racism and the failure to understand this continues to quietly propel the white supremacism that, thanks largely to the 'free' press described above, has wormed its way back into Western discourse in recent years.

Because the plight of the Palestinian people is so dire, because my Catholic teachers were still casually explaining how 'the Jews killed Jesus' in the 1980s and because, as with my Nigerian cousins, my early encounters with Jewish people did not admit the realities of the racism they might face, I arrived on air in my early thirties unpersuaded that anti-Semitism even existed in any meaningful sense. Given that I was born so shortly after the Holocaust ended, that is an objectively astonishing conclusion to have arrived at, but it is far from a rare one.

Anti-Semitism does not 'feel' like racism to many because Jewish people are routinely portrayed as 'powerful'. That this portrayal, whether on murals celebrated on Facebook or in barely veiled diatribes about George Soros or 'globalists', is itself the oldest anti-Semitic trope of all gets lost in translation. I took a call shortly after Jeremy Corbyn became leader of the Labour Party from a well-spoken middle-class woman in her early twenties. 'It is not anti-Semitic to say that the Jews control the media,' she told me. 'Because they do.'

So it is that *any* criticism of Israel reaches *some* Jewish ears with a horrific shock. And so it is that well-meaning if ill-informed people like me can end up accused of anti-Semitism despite seeing ourselves as champions of the oppressed everywhere. Israel is the place to which Jewish people can flee *when it starts happening again* and it is, in my considered opinion, absolutely impossible to separate this fact from the broader contemplations. It is both a country and a state of mind. When I criticise the Occupied Territories or detail the dizzying difference in death tolls or even compare the ordnance flying in one direction to the ordnance flying in the other, I am not just making objective observations about events. I am threatening the existence of the place in which all Jewish people can seek sanctuary *when it starts happening again*. Of all the lessons I have learned from my callers over the years this has perhaps been the hardest. Even relatively recently, while railing against Donald Trump's so-called Muslim ban, I was comprehensively 'schooled' about the number of Arab countries where Israeli citizens are not permitted to travel.

We may one day inhabit a world where there is no danger of *it* happening again, but until we do it seems to me profoundly wrong to see Israel in exactly the same way that we see other countries. I will continue to criticise policies and politicians but always with two thoughts, sown and grown by my listeners over the years, in the forefront of my mind: are you focusing more attention on the things you dislike about Israel's policies than you are on the things you dislike about, say, Russia's or America's – and if so, why? And are you being fully cognisant of the fact that for many people listening to you right now Israel is the place to which they will flee *when it starts happening again*?

I hope, but can't be sure, that there was never any outright bullying involved when I clashed with callers whose support for Israel seemed to me to be blind. I know that I have often reached for the bully's toolbox on other issues over the years. Vegetarianism and veganism provide perhaps the best examples. I can say now that my historic mockery of vegetarians, though ostensibly affectionate, was born of shame and guilt. I still eat meat, by the way, but I share my home with two people who don't and it was my youngest daughter's quiet confidence that eating flesh was just wrong that first alerted me to the error of my ways.

I had previously thought it was funny to tease people like her, to make light of their deeply held convictions and even to point out facetiously that we had offered a vegetarian option at our wedding while our vegetarian friends had not felt similarly compelled to offer meat dishes at theirs. I would argue, quite seriously, that vegetarianism entailed blatant hypocrisy because people who professed to be passionately opposed to the killing of calves or chickens rarely objected to the killing of cockroaches or rats. I even reached regularly for the old canard about their leather shoes making a mockery of their principles. I remember this now every time we embark on the epic quest to find vegan school shoes for my daughter.

Around the time she became vegetarian, I was discussing some footage of a fox hunter battering a hunt saboteur that had been widely reported. Shortly after I had trotted out my usual self-congratulatory bilge about 'so-called' animal rights activists being unbothered by pest control, Laura rang in. It was a memorable exchange.

Laura: I sabotage rat traps all the time!

James: How do you sabotage a rat trap?

Laura: Break them. Smash them up. Throw them away. If I see any trap for any animal, it goes.

James: And my friend whose son nearly died after contracting Weil's disease from rat urine – how would you explain your behaviour to him?

Laura: If an animal being responsible for somebody's illness and death warrants the death of that animal then what do humans deserve for killing 152 billion animals every year on this planet?

James: You're conflating humanity with the animal world, which you're perfectly entitled to do, but you don't get to take anyone else with you when you do. Otherwise, you'd be arguing that you should be allowed to marry a horse, like Caligula. [This is not just daft but also historically inaccurate but I realised neither at the time. As usual, I was so desperate to 'win' the argument that I was already lobbing everything at it.]

Laura: That doesn't make any sense.

James: It makes exactly as much sense as your attempt to say that if an animal gets killed for killing a human then all the humans should get killed for killing animals.

Laura: I didn't say that.

James: It's a moral equivalence and I don't see an animal killing a human and a human killing an animal as remotely equivalent things. Keeping vermin away from human dwellings is an intrinsic part of civilisation.

Laura: But the animals were there first. We have this with foxes too and I did notice you say earlier – and I understand it – that if someone has lambs or chickens and a fox comes and kills them then straight away you'll want to kill that fox, but the fox was just doing what comes naturally. You should protect your livestock better.

James: Isn't it natural to kill and eat animals?

Laura: No, it's not. We're actually obligate herbivores.

James: But in the sense of statistical popularity it's just normal to eat meat.

Laura: You use the word normal; in clinical psychology terms it's actually psychopathic.

James: It's psychopathic to eat meat?

Laura: Not to eat meat but to kill animals.

James: (sounding very pleased with myself) Surely you'd want me to kill it first, though? You wouldn't rather I took a bite out of a living thing?

Laura: Actually, if you want to call yourself a carnivore then you need to track down a squirrel in the street and eat it raw, eat it live as any other mammal would in nature. Only then would I not have a problem with you eating meat.

James: Crikey. Do you get invited to a lot of dinner parties, Laura?

Laura: I throw a lot of dinner parties and my vegan friends come round and we laugh about people who eat corpses.

James: (laughing) So I'm a corpse-munching psychopath now?

Laura: (laughing) Yes!

James: I don't think we're going to agree about this but thank you for keeping things friendly.

Laura is, obviously, notably uncompromising in her beliefs but she did something to me that I often boast about doing to others. By articulating her principles and the grounds for her convictions, she holds up a mirror to my own and leaves me with a simple choice: acknowledge the paucity and weakness of my own position or attack the person holding up the mirror in the hope of sustaining the delusion that I am not in the wrong.

This is not to suggest that I think she was right about everything but if you feel even the vaguest warmth toward any animal you will know, somewhere deep inside, that eating other ones is morally and intellectually indefensible. How, for example, can it be alright to eat a pig but not a dog? A chicken but not a hamster? As soon as you start thinking deeply about these issues it becomes impossible to sustain a consistent position and this is why we mostly elect never to think too deeply about them.

But if you are living in a state of permanent hypervigilance – if you can't take your armour off – then you don't have that freedom. You have to attack the person who is making you feel bad. You might not realise that your 'comical' antipathy toward vegans is a result of the shame and guilt they make you feel about your own behaviour and beliefs but it incontrovertibly is. How else can you explain the way in which some professional gobs on sticks took such grave offence when the bakery chain Greggs introduced a vegan sausage roll in 2019? Not instead of a meat product, not to replace pork sausage rolls, but as an *addition* to the range. They need to denigrate vegetarians and vegans because the alternative is to own their own wrongness.

The comedian and director Simon Amstell, in his most excellent film *Carnage: Swallowing the Past*, posits a fictional future in which eating flesh has become such a disgusting concept that nobody can quite understand how humans ever did it. I've watched the film, I've spoken with Simon, I've watched family members embrace vegetarianism without any preachiness or sententiousness and I still eat meat. Why? Because I am not as moral or as honest or as compassionate as they are. I am wrong. They are right. Admitting this once again makes me a hypocrite but it is, as I said, a work in progress and I hope that being a hypocrite is better than being a bully.

I'm going to close with another animal-related example of my wrongness that has haunted me for years. I felt something shift inside me when it happened and it has never shifted back again. Of all the stories in this book it may well be the most trivial, the most seemingly innocuous, but it is also, I think, the most human.

Once again as a sort of performative provocativeness, I used to enjoy mocking people whose affection for their pets seemed to be greater than their affection for other people. I don't think there was any shame or guilt involved in my position this time, I just thought it was funny to laugh at them. I was, in other words, bullying people but excusing myself on the grounds that it made other people laugh. It's hard to quantify how much modern comedy relies on this, and many performers and

writers I admire greatly are articulate and adamant that policing offence is dangerous and wrong. I'm not so sure any more.
Instead of arguing about whether or not we should be able to
malign and insult vulnerable groups, for laughs and with impunity, I find myself wondering more and more about why anyone would need to. The distinction between beliefs, which
absolutely have to be subject to scrutiny and mockery, and
immutable characteristics, which should not, seems dangerously blurred. Again, the trans issue has contributed to the
confusion.

I had never owned a dog and it was dog owners at whom I
directed the bulk of my bile. Excessive affection for canines, I
argued at the time, is evidence of an inability to build meaningful relationships with humans. It speaks of a refusal to reach
the sort of compromise that friendly relations demand. I would
'tease' offended callers by asking how long they would have to
lie dead on their sofa before their dog started eating them and,
in response, they would oscillate between hurt and outrage.
And then an email dropped into my inbox while I was banging
on again about the emotional stuntedness of people who loved
their pets 'too much'. It arrived in the month of June.

Dear James,

My wife of 54 years died in January and if it wasn't for the
company of our two Dachshunds I know I could not have
endured the pain of losing her. Your radio show has also been

a great source of comfort and company to me over the last few months. Please think of me next time you are discussing owners who perhaps seem excessively fond of their dogs.

Yours sincerely,

Dennis

It took me years to realise that the most important part of being a broadcaster is not how you speak but how you listen. It took me roughly the same amount of time to see that what I thought were strengths could be weaknesses. I now know that almost all of our most toxic attitudes towards blameless, innocent people are born of buried pain, shame and guilt about ourselves and our own experiences, but it took me a long time. I have finally learned that admitting to being wrong is infinitely more important than using skills and tricks and weapons and tools to look 'right', and that there is no point having a mind if you never change it.

Better late than never.

A NOTE ON THE TEXT

I HAVE TRIED WHEREVER possible to reproduce on-air conversations verbatim and every effort has been made to reflect original conversations as they happened. However, some names and details have been changed to protect the innocent.

A NOTE ON THE TEXT

ACKNOWLEDGEMENTS

WITH THANKS TO: JAMIE Joseph, Liz Marvin, John Gilbert, Joanna Bennett, Caroline Butler and everyone behind the scenes at Penguin. To: Laelia Hartnoll, Julie L E, Aurelie C, Adrian Sherling, Sam Dayeh, Ava Evans, Keith True, John Chittenden, Ciara Parkes, Scott Balcony, Gary Burton, Wayne Lynch, Emrys Myrddin, Emma Ko, Nils Sjöberg, Ben Elias, and Matthew Torbitt. With thanks for leaning in: Rae McDonald & David Lewis, Charlotte O'Brien, Claire McDonald & Liam Plowman, Rufus & Bruno, Jennifer Park, Lara & Andy Taylor, Jane & Charles Kingsmill, Judit Bogdan, Kerry & Jason Farrell, Jane & Bob Suppiah, Alice Suppiah, Andreas & Sophie Georghiou, Jonny Crowe, Maria G, Vanessa & Tobyn Andreae, Susannah Rustin & Ludo Hunter-Tilney, Susan & Dara, Maggie Terefenko, Eliza Cagnino, Amy J S and Farida Mannan.

Finally, with thanks for pretty much everything, to Lucy McDonald.